15 Things Happening in Japan

From〈A Hit Drama "Hanzawa Naoki"〉

to〈Yoshitomo Nara's New Life〉

SHOHAKUSHA

はじめに

本書はアメリカの有力経済紙『ウォール・ストリート・ジャーナル』(The Wall Street Journal, WSJ) の東京支局の記者が「いま一番新しい日本」を世界に向けてリポートするブログサイトJapan Real Time(JRT)のコーナーで連載している記事を題材にしています。JRTの記事は、エキゾチックなベールで日本を覆った思わせぶりなものでも、クールジャパンのイメージを表面的になぞるものでも、ありません。JRTのスタンスは、サブカルチャーからシリアスな社会現象まで、縦横無尽に分析を加え、時に歴史を紐解きながら、その背景と全体像を描き出すものです。

皆さんは「カワイイ」、「半沢直樹」から「東日本大震災」、「原発問題」まで、身近にある事柄を、本書を通じて、さらに深く広く知ることができるようになります。

本書の使い方

Matching Words & Phrases

これから読む本文に出てくる重要な単語やフレーズにふさわしい日本語の語義を選ぶ問題です。鍵となる語彙の意味を頭に入れておくことで、スムーズに本文を読むことができるようになります。

Reading Passages

500語前後の英語で書かれた、TBSドラマ『半沢直樹』、福岡の屋台文化など、他にはない魅力的なラインナップです。重要な語句や難易度が高い語句は側注で意味が確認できるようになっています。なお、countableの名詞の場合でもa/-sは省略しています。また、確実に学習してほしい文法事項や内容のより詳しい説明などは、すぐ後のThe Keys to Reading Passagesで記しています。側注とThe Keys to Reading Passagesの助けを借り、本文の内容を把握しましょう。

Checking Your Understanding: True or False

本文の内容について書かれた英文が正しいかどうかを判断する問題です。まずテキストを一通り読み、概要が正しく把握できているのかどうかを確認しましょう。

How to Read a Paragraph

答えのヒントが書かれているパラグラフ番号を記してあります。本文中の当該パラグラフをもう一度よく読んで問題に答えましょう。

Translating into English

本文に出てきた文章の単語を並び替える英作文問題です。本文を見ずに、提示された日本語のみを参考にしながら並び替えましょう。

Listening Summary

本文の英語の要約の穴埋め問題です。本文全体の意味を大まかに掴んでいることが重要です。その上で文法や意味を考え、選択肢の中からふさわしい単語を選びましょう。また、音声を使用して答え合わせもできますから、リスニング能力の向上にも役立ちます。

Contents

UNIT

1 5 Things You Didn't Know About Kawaii

Kawaii の美学

Photo, Designed by Takuya Angel

「カワイイ」はキュート（cute）だけれど、キュート過ぎてはいけない――と言われてピンと来るだろうか？　うなずいたあなたはカワイイの美学（aesthetic）が分かっている人だ。日本発の kawaii は今や世界に向けて発信され、受け入れられている。その証拠に kawaii は既に英語となっているのだ。しかし kawaii を一言で説明するのは難しい。多種多様な場面でお目にかかり（multiple examples）、時に矛盾する複数の概念（conflicting views）を持つ、知っているようで知らない、kawaii のディープな美学や歴史を探ってみよう。

Matching Words & Phrases

次の 1 ～ 10 の語句を、ⓐ ～ⓙの中の最も適切な意味と線で結びましょう。

1. encounter	・	ⓐ はっきりと分かる
2. know	・	ⓑ（歴史・政治上の）時代 ★普通 age より短い。
3. dominant	・	ⓒ（思いがけなく）…に出会う
4. deal in	・	ⓓ（…の範囲内に）限定する
5. otherwise	・	ⓔ（数・度合い・影響力などが）際立っている
6. abound	・	ⓕ（人・態度などが）…の意味を含む
7. adapt to	・	ⓖ（人が）…を扱う
8. era	・	ⓗ（物・生物が）たくさんある
9. imply	・	ⓘ（…を必要・状況などに）適合・適応させる
10. confine to	・	ⓙ もしそうでなければ

Reading Passages

[1] If you've ever been to Japan, whether you know it or not, you will have encountered multiple examples of *kawaii*, the country's dominant pop-cultural aesthetic.

[2] That bus stop shaped like a watermelon? Kawaii. 5 Adorable police mascots? Kawaii. Harajuku fashionistas with pink tutus and purple bangs, Hello Kitty TV sets, fish cakes that look like pandas, girls in manga with sparkly eyes, construction signs that take the form of frogs? All kawaii.

10 [3] Kawaii culture has many guises, but what exactly is it? If it's just the Japanese word for "cute," as it's usually translated, why not just call it that?

[4] In my book, *Kawaii!: Japan's Culture of Cute*, I spoke to product designers, manga artists, fashion luminaries, event 15 organizers, scholars and artists who deal in kawaii. One thing they made clear is that contrary to popular belief, kawaii products need to be cute, but not *too* cute–otherwise they won't sell.

[5] Conflicting views abound as to what kawaii is and isn't. 20 In light of this, below are five things about kawaii that go against common misperceptions. I hope they help you look at kawaii in a different light.

[6] **1. Kawaii isn't about perfection**

Though kawaii design is usually associated with a 25 roundness of composition, pastel colors and childlike facial proportions, aesthetic perfection is actually undesirable. Kazuhiko Hachiya, the designer of character goods PostPet, points out that if characters are too perfect, consumers greet them suspicion and unease. That explains why his hit 30 kawaii characters, Momo and friends, have asymmetrical poses and aren't immaculately cute.

[7] **2. Kawaii isn't anything new**

Kawaii culture developed largely as a result of the convergence of traditions adapting to modern times, and the 35 appropriation and influence of Western culture, particularly after World War II. But its roots go even deeper: Many people consider its birth to be the beginning of the Taisho era (1912-1926), when designer Takehisa Yumeji made

adorable:「可愛らしい」
guise:「外見、見かけ」
for:「…を表すものとして」
why not ...?:「なぜ…してはいけないのか、…してもよいではないか」
contrary to ...:「…に反する」
as to ...:「…に関して」
misperception:「誤解」
light:「見方、観点」
undesirable:「望ましくない」
point out:「指摘する」
greet:「(〜な態度で)接する」
asymmetric(al):「左右非対称な」
immaculately:「完璧に」
as a result of:「…の結果として」
convergence:「一点に集まること、収れん」
appropriation:「流用」

feminine items specifically marketed toward girls.

40 [8] **3. Kawaii isn't supposed to be sexy**

In the 1990s, with the rise of Harajuku youth fashion and the influence of *shojo* (girls) manga and illustrators, kawaii became an ideal, something girls wanted to be. Rather than be pretty, sexy or glamorous, Japanese girls prefer to be 45 called kawaii. As an adjective, the word commonly implies that something or someone is cute, sweet, endearing and innocent, but it can be used in a mind-boggling array of ways. In fact, girls in Japan will exclaim "kawaii!" so many times a day, and apply it in so many different contexts–often 50 ironic–that to a foreigner it may seem like their repertoire in vocabulary is somewhat limited!

[9] **4. Kawaii isn't static**

While kawaii culture has been around in Japan for roughly a hundred years, it is constantly mutating into new 55 directions, thus retaining its appeal to a fickle consumer demographic. Increasingly, kawaii is teamed with words that might seem like its antithesis: take *ero-kawaii* (erotic cute), *kimo-kawaii* (creepy cute) and *guro-kawaii* (grotesque cute). In the past five years or so, hit products such as 60 Gloomy, a pink homicidal bear often depicted attacking his owner, are the opposite of what we might commonly consider cute.

[10] **5. Kawaii isn't confined to Japan**

These days it isn't just Japanese people that have an all- 65 encompassing love of kawaii: fans of the culture are popping up globally, from the Japan Expo in Paris, HARAJUKU KAWAii!! at London's HYPER JAPAN event, and San Francisco's J-Pop Summit Festival. As for whether it will become more than a subculture overseas, we'll have to wait 70 and see.

be supposed to ...：「…であると考えられる」
ideal:「理想、お手本」
prefer to be / do:「…を好む」
apply:「使う」
ironic:「矛盾する」
be teamed with ... :「…と組み合わせる」
antithesis :「…の正反対(のもの)」
creepy:「気味の悪い」
homicidal:「人を殺したいという衝動を持つ」
depict:「(絵画等によって)描写する」
all-encompassing:「すべてを網羅するような」
globally:「世界的に」
as for ... :「…については」
wait and see:「成り行きを見守る」

The Keys to Reading Passages

l. 5 ……… **adorable**　kawaii に近接した意味をもつ単語を確認しよう。adorable は「愛らしい」、cute は「(女性や子供など小さなものに対して、並外れてはいないが) 可愛い」という意味だが、北米では「(性的に) 魅力的な」という意味を含むことがある。sweet は「(性質・作法が) 感じの良い、好感の持てる」、endearing は「人から愛情を引出すような」という意味。

l. 10-12 … **2nd paragraph**　ここでは「これはどうだろう？」―「カワイイ」と質疑応答形式でカワイイの例を読者に提示している。また、「ピンクのチュチュを着て紫の前髪をした原宿のファッションリーダーたち」、「漫画の中に登場する輝く瞳の少女たち」等、カワイイと結びつきやすいものと並んで、「さつま揚げ」(fish cakes)、家電や「工事中の標識」(construction signs) といった実用的なものも、カワイイものと化して、日本の日常の風景に溶け込んでいることに注目したい。

l. 11 …… **for**　よく使われる次の表現も覚えよう。A stands for B「B の意味を表す A」 Ex. The UN stands for the United Nations.「UN は国際連合の略である」

l. 16 …… **contrary to**　**on the contrary** と **to the contrary** も合わせて覚えよう。

- on the contrary :「これに反して、それどころか」Ex. "You look tired." "On the contrary, I feel fine."「疲れているみたいだね。」「それどころか、とっても元気だよ。」
- to the contrary :「それと反対に、そうではなく」Ex. I believe he is innocent, whatever they may say to the contrary.「彼が無実だと信じている。彼らが反対のことを言おうとだ。」

l. 33 …… **result**　後に in か from が来るかで意味が反対になるので一緒に覚えよう。result in ...「…の結果になる」、result from ...「…という原因から生じる」

l. 43-45 … **Rather than be pretty, ... prefer to be**　倒置が起きている。元の語順は "... prefer to be ... rather than ..." となる。

l. 44 …… **prefer to**　prefer A to B「B より A が好き」も覚えよう。比較対象を表すとき通常は than を使うが、prefer には to を使うことにも注意。

l. 48-51 … **so ... that ~ 構文**　so ... that ~「…なので～である」となる、すなわち In fact, girls ... limited! の一文は「実際、少女達は一日に何回も「カワイイ！」と叫び…なので、外国人には彼女達の語彙のレパートリーがやや乏しいと映る」という意味。

Checking Your Understanding: True or False

本文の内容に照らして合っているものにはTを、間違えているものにはFを書きなさい。

1. ___ Consumers greet PostPet characters comfortablely because they are perfectly cute.

2. ___ The beginning of the Taisho era is said to be the origin of the kawaii culture.

3. ___ In fact, girls in Japan say "kawaii" many times a day because they have poor vocabulary.

4. ___ Kawaii culture is appealing to people all over the world, because it has kept its tradition for around one hundred years.

How to Read a Paragraph

以下の問いに答えなさい。なお、（　）内は正解が記述されている段落番号です。

1. 「カワイイ」は cute でありながらも、cute とは決定的に違うと述べられています。どう違うのかを説明しなさい。(Paragraph 4)

____

2. カワイイ文化のルーツとして、竹久夢二は何をしたか説明しなさい。(Paragraph 7)

____

3. カワイイ文化が消費者を引きつけてきた理由には、常にカワイイ文化自体が変化し続けたことが挙げられます。その例を挙げなさい。(Paragraph 9)

____

Translating into English

Reading Passeges を見ずに、日本語に合うように（　　　）内の語句を並び替えて、英文を完成させましょう。冒頭に来る語でも頭文字を小文字にしてあります。

1. これを考慮に入れて、以下は一般的な誤解に真っ向から対立するカワイイについての５つの事柄である。
   In light of this, (kawaii / five / about / common / go / things / below / that / against / misperceptions / are).

   ____

2. カワイイデザインはたいてい丸みを帯びた構図、パステルカラーや子どものような顔の均整などと結びつけて考えられる。
   Kawaii design is (with / a roundness / composition / associated / of / usually), (proportions / pastel colors / facial / childlike / and).

   ____

3. カワイイ文化は飽きっぽい消費者たちに対してその魅力を保持してきた。
   (culture / a / been / kawaii / has / fickle / to / appeal / consumer / its / demographic / retaining).

   ____

Listening Summary

下記の単語から正しいものを選んで空欄を埋めなさい。また、音声を聴いて答えを確認しましょう。

Kawaii, which has many different ①(　　　　　　　　　), ②(　　　　　　　　　) in Japan so you cannot say kawaii ③(　　　　　　　　　) just one word in English, for example, cute or ④(　　　　　　　　　). In addition, kawaii culture is ⑤(　　　　　　　　　) into new ways. However, one clear thing is that kawaii products should not be ⑥(　　　　　　　　　) cute– ⑦(　　　　　　　　　) it loses the essence of kawaii.

• otherwise • mutating • adorable • abounds • guises • for • too

UNIT

2 Uniqlo Finds Wealth of Data in Bangladesh Not-For-Profit Venture

ユニクロが蓄積したお宝データ

写真：ロイター / アフロ

安い労働力を求めて東南アジアに工場を移すという話は良く聞くが、ユニクロにとっては、安さよりバングラデシュで蓄積した（accumulating）データの方がお宝（wealth）ほどの価値がある（invaluable）。中国や東南アジアといったこれから伸びてくる市場（emerging markets）に食い込んでいくために役立つからだ。ユニクロはムハマド・ユヌス氏が創立したグラミンヘルスケアトラスト（Grameen Healthcare Trust）と手を組み NPO の合弁事業（a joint venture）を立ち上げた。マイクロファイナンスのグラミン銀行のメリットを活かして、バングラデシュの人々でもユニクロの商品を購入できる仕組みを作り、さらに消費者行動の貴重なデータを蓄積していく。その仕組みとは、そのデータとは──。

Matching Words & Phrases

次の 1 ～ 10 の語句を、ⓐ ～ⓙの中の最も適切な意味と線で結びましょう。

1. affordable	ⓐ …の発達を促進する、はぐくむ
2. profitable	ⓑ（特定メーカーの）系列小売店
3. exploit	ⓒ（商売などが）利益になる
4. nurture	ⓓ（業績・生産などで）先行する
5. stumble on	ⓔ 偶然見つける
6. overtake	ⓕ 約束する
7. outlet	ⓖ 検査、点検
8. erupt	ⓗ（暴行行為・争いなどが）勃発する
9. pledge	ⓘ 搾取する、不当に利益を得る
10. inspection	ⓙ（値段などが）手の届く範囲の

Reading Passages

1 In Bangladesh's villages and on its street corners, Japanese fashion giant Uniqlo is quietly gathering market data to help it in its ambition of becoming the world's top clothing brand in seven years.

2 Like other global brands, Uniqlo set up shop in Bangladesh's cities to tap into their cheap labor and make casual fashion wear affordable and profitable. But it has also gone into the country's impoverished villages and neighborhoods looking for a way to give something back to a country that many said was being exploited by the garment industry.

3 In 2010, Uniqlo formed a joint venture with Grameen Healthcare Trust, a not-for-profit organization created by Nobel laureate Muhammad Yunus, founder of the microfinance organization Grameen Bank.

4 The purpose of Grameen Uniqlo is to sell clothes made by locals, for locals, at affordable prices for people living near the poverty line, and to nurture local retailing expertise. But as the local retail staff diligently tallied their door-to-door sales of T-shirts, priced at $1 or $2, from village to village, the company that owns Uniqlo, Fast Retailing Co., realized it had stumbled on a wealth of untapped data on a rapidly growing economy.

5 "We learned which communities craved bright reds and greens, which preferred muted tones," Fast Retailing Senior Vice President Yukihiro Nitta said in an interview. "We learned to stock more men's wear, because women who wear saris buy mostly leggings and home wear."

6 When the venture opened its first stores in Dhaka in July, Mr. Nitta discovered that in a shop full of $2 and $3 items, shoppers will spend $10 for a pair of jeans or $9 for a shirt with a collar that can be used on more formal occasions. The stores now stock 70% to 75% of a store's floor space with items for men.

7 Fast Retailing—whose global empire is expanding at a breakneck clip of almost 20 stores a week—is looking for any edge it can use to overtake bigger rivals Gap Inc., Hennes & Mauritz AB and Inditex SA. Fast Retailing's

ambition:「野望」
tap into :「利用する」
impoverished:「貧困に陥った」
garment industry:「衣料品産業」
retailing:「小売業」
expertise:「専門知識」
tally:「集計する」
untapped:「まだ利用されていない」
crave:「…を欲する」
muted tones:「抑えた色味」
stock [動]:「(在庫として)ある」
sari:「(衣服の)サリー」
Dhaka:「ダッカ(バングラデシュの首都)」
formal occasion:「フォーマルな機会」
at a breakneck clip:「猛スピードで」
edge:「強み」

billionaire chief executive Tadashi Yanai aims to make the
40 company the world's biggest clothing retailer by 2020, with his focus on China, Southeast Asia and emerging markets.

8 "Bangladesh is extremely attractive as a market, not just as a production hub," Mr. Nitta said. "The know-how we are accumulating will be invaluable as the economy grows. It's
45 also a great resource as we expand throughout Asia."

9 Each Grameen Uniqlo outlet in Dhaka is a fraction of the size of the mammoth Uniqlo outlets in Shanghai or New York, but the network is growing. The venture will open two more stores on the first weekend of October, doubling
50 its stores there in less than three months. Fast Retailing envisions a nationwide chain in three or four years. The stores plow all profits back into running and expanding the venture.

10 The venture's growth in Dhaka follows the tragic collapse
55 in April of the Rana Plaza garment complex, in which more than 1,100 workers died. Demonstrations erupted around the country, resulting in the closure of hundreds of clothing factories outside Dhaka last week.

11 Fast Retailing, which says it wasn't affected by the
60 closures, signed a legally binding labor-safety accord in Bangladesh in August, pledging more transparent inspections and oversight of fire and safety standards.

billionaire:「億万長者」
chief executive:「社長」
hub:「拠点」
fraction:「ごく小さい」
double[動]:「倍にする」
envision:「もくろむ」
plow:「(利益などを)投資する」
collapse:「(建物などの)倒壊」
demonstration:「デモ、抗議運動」
closure:「閉鎖」
oversight:「監視」

The Keys to Reading Passages

l. 2 ……… **Uniqlo** 「ユニクロ」日本のアパレルメーカーであるファーストリテイリング(Fast Retailing) が展開するブランド名。

l. 13 …… **not-for-profit organization** 「NPO」非営利で社会活動や慈善活動などを行う団体のこと。non-profit organization と同義。

l. 14 …… **Nobel laureate Muhammad Yunus, ... Grameen Bank.** 「ノーベル平和賞受賞者ムハマド･ユヌス氏、マイクロファイナンスのグラミン銀行の創始者」「マイクロファイナンス」とは通常の銀行が融資を拒否するような貧者に小口の融資などを行い､自力で貧困から脱することを目指す金融サービス。ユヌス(1940-)は経済博士でバングラデシュにて教鞭をとっていたが、貧しい人々が高利貸しへの返済で苦しんでいるのを目の当たりにして、1976 年、後のグラミン銀行につながる無担保少額融資のプロジェクトを始める。グラミン銀行（1983 年創立）は「貧者の銀行」とも呼ばれている。ユヌスは 2006 年ノーベル平和賞受賞。

l. 18 …… **the poverty line** 「貧困線」世界銀行の HP によれば「国際貧困ライン」を 1 日 1.25 ドル以下で暮らす人々と定義している。

l. 31 …… **a pair of jeans** 「ジーンズ一本」cf. a pair of glasses「眼鏡一個」/ a pair of pajamas「パジャマ一着」

l. 37-38 … **Gap Inc., Hennes & Mauritz AB and Inditex SA** 「ギャップ（アメリカ最大のアパレルメーカー）」､「へネス＆マウリッツ（スウェーデンのアパレルメーカーで H&M ブランドを展開している）」､「インディテックス（スペインのアパレルメーカーで Zara などのブランドを展開している）」

l. 54-55 … **the tragic collapse in April of the Rana Plaza garment complex** 2013 年 4 月 24 日、首都ダッカ近郊のビル「ラナプラザ」が倒壊し、1,100 人以上の死者が出た事故。当時、ビルには 5 つの縫製工場が入っていた。もともと 5 階建てのビルに建て増しして 8 階建てにした。

l. 60 …… **a legally binding labor-safety accord** 「法的拘束力のある労働安全協定」accord はここでは「協定」だが、他に「調和」「一致」などの意味がある。

Checking Your Understanding: True or False

本文の内容に照らして合っているものにはTを、間違えているものにはFを書きなさい。

1. ___ The original purpose of Grameen Uniqlo is to gather market data in Bangladesh.

2. ___ What the most valuable wealth Fast Retailing gets is the accumulation of data derived from its marketing activities in Bangladesh.

3. ___ Uniqlo regards Bangladesh just as an attractive production hub.

4. ___ Demonstrations broke out everywhere in Bangladesh after the collapse of the Rana Plaza. As a result, Fast Retailing Co., promised local workers to establish a safer working environment.

How to Read a Paragraph

以下の問いに答えなさい。なお、（　）内は正解が記述されている段落番号です。

1. グラミンユニクロの設立目的は何ですか。(Paragraph 4)

____

2. グラミンユニクロがダッカに一号店をオープンした時、どのようなデータを得ることができましたか。(Paragraph 6)

____

3. ファーストリテイリングにとって、生産力の強化および地元への利益の還元以外にバングラデシュに出店する利点とは何ですか。(Paragraph 8)

____

Translating into English

Reading Passeges を見ずに、日本語に合うように（　　　）内の語句を並び替えて、英文を完成させましょう。

1. ユニクロはバングラデシュの安い労働力を利用し、カジュアル衣料を手の届く価格で販売し、かつ利益のあがる事業にするためにバングラデシュの都市に出店した。

   Uniqlo set up shop in Bangladesh's cities to (their / into / labor / tap / cheap) and (casual / profitable / fashion / affordable / wear / and / make).

   ____

2. ユニクロは貧困に陥っているバングラデシュの村や地域に進出し、国（バングラデシュ）になにかお返しする方法を模索している。

   Uniqlo (impoverished / gone / country's / into / the / has / villages / and / neighborhoods) looking for a way to give something back to the country.

   ____

3. 店舗は全利益をその運転資金と事業拡大のために投資している。

   The stores (back / expanding / all / the / profits / into / running / plow / and / venture).

   ____

Listening Summary

下記の単語から正しいものを選んで空欄を埋めなさい。また、音声を聴いて答えを確認しましょう。

The purpose of Grameen Uniqlo is to sell clothes made by ①(　　　　　　　　), for locals, at ②(　　　　　　　　) prices for those who live in the ③(　　　　　　　　) villages as well as to ④(　　　　　　　　) local retailing knowledge. Unexpectedly, the Fast Retailing Co., found it ⑤(　　　　　　　　) ⑥(　　　　　　　　) a ⑦(　　　　　　　　) of untapped data which would be very useful to expand its business in other developing countries.

• **affordable** • **on** • **wealth** • **locals** • **stumbled** • **nurture** • **impoverished**

UNIT

3 When the B List Is Best

味が勝負のB級グルメ

© gori910 / PIXTA(ピクスタ)

B級グルメ（B-kyuu grume or B-grade groumet）とはごく庶民的な食べ物を味わうこと（an appreciation of food in its more common forms）であり、形式（style）や気取り（pretension）もなく、味がすべてだ。海外にもグルメを唸らす職人技のピクルスが載ったホットドッグ（gourmet hotdogs with artisanal pickles）などB級グルメの仲間（cousins）がいる。ただ決定的に違うのは、B級グルメ文化には洗練させようという気がない（it doesn't seek to improve）点だ。食べ物のチョイスによって、人々が分類され（labeled）細分化され（categorized）政治性や価値などが判断される（politicized and judged）昨今、今だけはそんなことを忘れて、料理の味に集中して楽しもう。

Matching Words & Phrases

次の1～10の語句を、ⓐ～ⓙの中の最も適切な意味と線で結びましょう。

1. refer to	・	ⓐ（事実・意見などを）得意になって論じる
2. weigh in	・	ⓑ 鼻持ちならない上流気取り、（学芸・趣味などの）気取り
3. additive［名］	・	ⓒ …の側面において
4. snobbery	・	ⓓ（作業など）最初から
5. atmosphere	・	ⓔ 郊外
6. in aspects of	・	ⓕ 添加物
7. suburban	・	ⓖ（場所や状況などに漂う）雰囲気、ムード
8. district	・	ⓗ 地区、地域
9. provenance	・	ⓘ（主語が名詞などを）指す
10. from scratch	・	ⓙ 起源、出所

Reading Passages

1 Japan holds more Michelin stars than any other country, but its love of food isn't limited to fine dining. The Japanese phrase B-kyuu gurume (B-grade gourmet) refers to an appreciation of food in its more common forms, where style and pretension take a back seat, and flavor is everything.

2 The concept of B-kyuu gurume covers a wide range of simple foods: everything from dumplings, rice bowls and street food to potato chips, canned coffee and instant noodles. I've seen B-kyuu gurume reviews where food critics weigh in on microwave-ready meals from Japanese convenience stores.

3 Taking a connoisseur's approach to simple foods is not unique to Japan. Gourmet hotdogs with artisanal pickles, burgers from dry-aged wagyu and the like can be found in almost any Western country. But the one point that sets B-kyuu gurume apart from its cousins abroad is that, as a culture, it doesn't seek to improve. Rather, the aim is to accept and appreciate the taste of simple foods for what they are, whether they may be handmade and organic, or out of a packet and loaded with additives.

4 At a time where our food allegiances have become badges of honor, the B-kyuu gurume approach is a refreshing contrast to the cynical and judgmental world of food snobbery.

5 Osaka is arguably the spiritual home of B-kyuu gurume. The informal, extroverted and sociable atmosphere of Japan's second largest city is very different to the glamor of Tokyo and the elegance of Kyoto, and these characteristics of Osaka and its people are reflected in aspects of the local cuisine.

6 Simple dishes like okonomiyaki (a kind of cabbage pancake), takoyaki (octopus balls) and kushi-katsu (deep-fried skewers) are sold for just a few dollars all over Osaka. Often covered in sweet and salty sauces or streaked with mayonnaise, the flavors of many B-kyuu gurume favorites are not the subtle or delicate tastes more commonly associated with Japanese cuisine.

7 Last week I ate at Noboridako in Osaka's suburban Inada

be limited to:「…に限られる」
fine dining:「高級料理」
take a back seat:「二の次になる」
a wide range of ...:「幅広い…」
review:「批評、レビュー」
critics:「評論家」
microwave-ready meal:「レンジ調理食品」
connoisseur:「通、玄人」
dry-aged:「乾燥熟成させた」
set A apart from B:「AをBと比べて際立たせる」
out of a packet:「袋から出せば食べられる」
loaded with:「…を多く含む」
allegiance:「忠誠、執着」
refreshing:「胸のすくような」
judgmental:「批判的な」
extroverted:「社交的な」
sociable:「人懐っこい」
glamor:「魅力、魔力」
cuisine:「料理」
dish:「料理」
octopus:「たこ」
skewer:「焼き串」
be streaked with ...:「…の縞(しま)になっている」
subtle:「繊細な」

district, a hole-in-the-wall operated by Hiroko Wada and
40 her husband Shotaro. It has two tables, but most customers
order from a long service window that opens directly onto
the street. It specializes in takoyaki and okonomiyaki.

8 I was introduced to Noboridako by Kimiyasu Chiba,
a retired sumo wrestler who has been coming here for so
45 long he even has a few of his own creations on the menu.
Together, he and Mrs. Wada developed a unique takoyaki
topped with salt, ground sesame seeds and spring onions,
inspired by Mr. Chiba's sumo past. It's delicious, and lighter
than the standard takoyaki that is usually covered in a
50 thick, Worcestershire-like sauce.

9 Mrs. Wada's takoyaki is an example of B-kyuu gurume
at its best. She doesn't know what kinds of flours go into
her batter mix; she buys it premade and has been using the
same brand for decades because it produces just the right
55 texture. Nor does she know the provenance of the cabbage
for her okonomiyaki, which comes pre-shredded in vacuum
bags. She does make her own okonomiyaki sauce from
scratch, but that's just because she's never found a pre-made
sauce that's to her taste. Her food is cheap, unpretentious
60 and delicious.

10 Organic, sustainable, artisan, local, vegan, gluten-free, or
ethical—our food choices are becoming increasingly labeled,
categorized, politicized and judged. And so it's nice to take a
break from it all even for a moment, to forget nutrition, ego
65 and politics, and to enjoy a plate of food just for the way it
tastes.

hole-in-the-wall:「吹けば飛ぶような」
operate:「経営する」
open onto ... :「…に面している」
specialize in:「…を得意とする、…を売りとする」
retired:「引退した」
ground > grind:「すりつぶした」
inspired by ... :「…にインスピレーションを得る」
... at its best:「最高の…」
flour:「小麦粉」
for decades:「何十年もの間」
texture:「きめ」
vacuum bag:「真空パック」
to one's taste:「(しばしば否定文で)好みに合った」
unpretentious:「気取らない」

The Keys to Reading Passages

l. 1 ……… **Michelin stars** フランスのミシュランが作る食のガイドブック。1つ星から3つ星でレストランを評価している。1つ星でもミシュランに載るのは名誉なこととされている。

l. 7-9 …… **dumplings, rice bowls and street food to potato chips, canned coffee and instant noodles.** 「餃子、丼もの、屋台の食べ物からポテトチップス、缶コーヒーやインスタントヌードル」B級グルメの代表的なものが列記されており、下記で説明しているorganicなどとは正反対のフードチョイスである。(良いか悪いかは別として) 産地や栄養などに無頓着だったり、添加物たっぷりの食べ物が並んでいる。

l.53 ……… **batter mix** 「(料理用の) バッター」batterは天ぷらの衣やお好み焼きの生地など、小麦粉や牛乳、卵など水でこねて混ぜたもの。ここでのbatter mixは粉状の材料があらかじめ配合されている (市販の) お好み焼き粉やたこ焼き粉などのミックス粉を指す。

l.55 ……… **Nor does she know ...** 「また彼女は…知らない」(おさらい) Nor V+S ／ So V+S で「また〜も…でない (否定) ／また〜も…である (肯定)」

l.61-62 … **Organic, sustainable, artisan, local, vegan, gluten-free, or ethical** organic「オーガニックの (有機農法で作られた)」、sustainable「地球に優しい」、artisan「職人の腕を存分にふるった」、local「地元で収穫された (地産地消の)」、vegan「ビーガンの (注：ビーガンは乳製品もとらない厳格な菜食主義者)」、gluten-free「(小麦などに含まれる) グルテンを含まない (注：グルテンはアレルギーを引き起こすことがあるとされている)」、ethical「倫理にかなった方法で調達された (注：発展途上国の生産者を搾取せず、正当な対価を支払って取引するフェアトレードなどが一例である)」

l. 64-65 … **nutrition, ego and politics** オーガニックなど上記に挙げた食を選択する行為は、どのような栄養をとるかということはもちろん、その行為自体がその人の自己を満したり、また政治性を表す指標になったりすることをここでは示唆している。

Checking Your Understanding: True or False

本文の内容に照らして合っているものにはTを、間違えているものにはFを書きなさい。

1. ___ Japan holds many Michelin stars because of its love of B-rating gourmet food.
2. ___ Western countries also enjoy B-rating gourmet food like hot dogs with artisanal pickles and burgers from dry-aged beef.
3. ___ A B-rating gourmet lover would prefer a simple taste to subtle and delicate tastes.
4. ___ B-rating gourmet food is not associated with one's political attitude.

How to Read a Paragraph

以下の問いに答えなさい。なお、（　）内は正解が記述されている段落番号です。

1. 日本のB級グルメの特徴とは何ですか。(Paragraph 3)

____

2. 大阪はどんな雰囲気だと述べられていますか。(Paragraph 5)

____

3. B級グルメと対極にある食文化の潮流について説明しなさい。(Paragraph 10)

____

Translating into English

Reading Passeges を見ずに、日本語に合うように（　　　）内の語句を並び替えて、英文を完成させましょう。冒頭に来る語でも頭文字を小文字にしてあります。

1. B 級グルメという日本語のフレーズはごく庶民的な形で食べ物を味わうことを指している。
   The Japanese phrase B-kyuu gurume (more / to / its / forms / an / of / food / in / common / refers / appreciation).

   ____

2. 大阪とその人々の特色が、その土地の料理にも現れている。
   The characteristics (local / its / people / are / in / cuisine / aspects / the / of / Osaka / reflected / of / and).

   ____

3. 彼女はまたお好み焼きに使っているキャベツの出所も知らない。
   (the / nor / of / cabbage / she / provenance / know / the / does) for her okonomiyaki.

   ____

Listening Summary

下記の単語から正しいものを選んで空欄を埋めなさい。また、音声を聴いて答えを確認しましょう。

B-kyuu gourmet food is different from its ①(　　　　　　　　) in Western countries in that it doesn't seek to ②(　　　　　　　　). The ③(　　　　　　　　) is to ④(　　　　　　　　) the taste of simple food rather than be cynical and judgmental as is often the case with the world of food ⑤(　　　　　　　　). Therefore, the informal and ⑥(　　　　　　　　) ⑦(　　　　　　　　) of Osaka makes it the spiritual home of B-rating gourmet food.

• **cousins** • **atmosphere** • **improve** • **snobbery** • **aim** • **appreciate** • **sociable**

UNIT

4 Harvard Degree: The Political Economy of Kumamon

くまモンの政治経済学

写真：AP/アフロ

熊本県（Kumamoto Prefecture）の営業部長（sales manager）くまモンが、県知事（Governor）の母校（alma mater）である名門ハーバード大学（Harvard University）から学位（degree）を授与――!? ハーバード大で蒲島知事は大勢の学部生（undergraduates）や大学院生（graduates）、教授らに迎えられ、くまモンはアメリカデビュー（debut）を果たした。知事は講演（seminar）でくまモンの成功戦略（strategy）は使用料無料（no-fee）とシンプルなデザインにあると語った。くまモンの肖像（image）を使いたければ、申請して（file for）許可（permission）を求めればいい。一方、過度な露出によって飽きられる（oversaturation）リスクも負っている（come with its own risks）と語る。

Matching Words & Phrases

次の 1 ～ 10 の語句を、ⓐ ～ⓙの中の最も適切な意味と線で結びましょう。

1. shift	・	ⓐ（他の意見・事例などを）引き合いに出す
2. duty	・	ⓑ 決まってすること、いつもの手順
3. proclaim	・	ⓒ（切に）…したがる
4. advocate	・	ⓓ 支持者
5. eager to	・	ⓔ 切り開く
6. modest	・	ⓕ 程よい、適度な
7. invoke	・	ⓖ 任務、職務
8. routine	・	ⓗ …への忠誠心
9. allegiance to	・	ⓘ（方向を）変える、移す
10. explore	・	ⓙ …を表明する

Reading Passages

1 CAMBRIDGE, Mass.—This has been a busy year for Kumamon. While continuing his duties as sales manager for Kumamoto Prefecture, Japan's favorite bear-like mascot became the first such character to meet the Emperor and Empress of Japan, and has taken his act overseas, to Taiwan and France.

2 Kumamon this week made his American debut. JRT caught up with him at Harvard University, where he was joined by his biggest fan and advocate, Governor Ikuo Kabashima of Kumamoto Prefecture.

3 In a seminar entitled "The Political Economy of Kumamon," Gov. Kabashima faced a packed lecture hall filled with more than 100 undergraduates, graduate students, and professors, and outlined his initiatives to explore new frontiers for Japan's public administration. "After the Lehman Crisis, I realized that we must shift values from economy to overall happiness," Gov. Kabashima said, invoking Kumamon as the key component to achieving happiness for the prefecture from which Kumamon derives his name. Halfway through the seminar, Kumamon swept in and jiggled through his routine, amidst laughter and claps from the audience.

4 For those who haven't yet caught up with the meteoric rise of Japan's new star: Kumamon was "born" in March, 2010, the lumpy bear-like brainchild of a governor eager to try out creative ways to promote tourism in Kumamoto. After a few redesigns (at first, his soft bodysuit was so frightening that children ran away from his looming black figure), the Kumamon character caught on throughout Japan. That wasn't just his cuteness, but the result of a clever "no-fee" strategy and a simple design. It does not cost money to use his image. A company just has to file for permission. And unlike other mascot characters in Japan, he is not decorated with items proclaiming his allegiance to a prefecture or a company—Kumamon is Kumamon, no strings attached.

5 Thus, his image can be seen everywhere, on hotel pillows, fake nails, chopping boards, packaging, planes, snacks, and

Mass.:「マサチューセッツ州」
such ... to do:「～するほどの…」
Emperor and Empress of Japan:「天皇陛下と皇后陛下」
entitled:「題した」
Gov.(=Governor):「知事」
filled with:「埋め尽くされた」
initiative:「構想、戦略」
new frontier:「新境地」
public administration:「行政」
component:「構成要素」
sweep in:「堂々と入ってくる」
jiggle:「軽く揺れる」
amidst:「…の真っただ中に」
meteoric rise:「彗星のごとき」
lumpy:「（塊りの意からここでは）メタボな」
looming:「不気味に迫ってくるような」
figure:「姿」
catch on:「流行する」
A is decorated with B:「AをBで飾り立てる」

books. According to a recent poll, 90% of Japanese people
40 say they recognize Kumamon, ranking him amongst such
icons as Hello Kitty, or Mickey Mouse.

6 But success comes with its own risks. In the seminar,
Gov. Kabashima said he was worried about oversaturation
of the mascot character within Japan. Overseas expansion
45 was the logical next step, hence Kumamon's travels to
Taiwan, France, and finally Harvard—the expansion of
what the governor fondly called "Kumamon Universe." Gov.
Kabashima told JRT he still has room to grow in the U.S.,
contrasting Kumamon's modest American reception with the
50 trip to Taiwan, where some fans waited seven hours to take
pictures with the mascot.

7 Harvard was a logical stop for Kumamon's American
tour. It's Gov. Kabashima's alma mater, having earned
a Ph.D. in political economy and government there in
55 1979. "I hope that Kumamon helps students consider new
possibilities in social and political activities, and risk new
frontiers in their lives," the governor said.

recent poll:「最近の世論調査」
amongst:=among
icon:「(熱愛や崇拝の対象になる)商品、アイコン」
overseas expansion:「海外進出」
hence:「従って」
fondly:「愛情を込めて」
reception:「反応」
stop:「訪問先」
earn a Ph.D:「博士課程を修了する」
risk[動]:「思い切ってやってみる」

The Keys to Reading Passages

l. 2-6 …… **While continuing ..., ... France.**　分詞構文に接続詞を残した構文。時や理由、条件や譲歩など表す従属節（副詞節）の接続詞と主語（主節の主語と一致している場合）を省略し、動詞を ... ing にするのが分詞構文。接続詞の意味を明確にしたいときに、接続詞残す場合がある。

l. 9-10 … **Ikuo Kabashima**　蒲島郁夫（1947- ）熊本県鹿本郡生まれの熊本県知事（任 2008- ）。高校卒業後、農協職員となりネブラスカ大学で農業研修の一環で畜産学を学ぶが、のちに政治学に転向しハーバード大学で博士号（政治経済博士 [Ph. D. in political economy and government]）を取得し、1997 年から東京大学法学部教授になった。同大学辞職後に現職に就任する。蒲島氏の経歴から、同氏の講演の言葉通り "risk new frontiers"「あえて新境地に挑む」を地で行く人物と言える。

l. 16 …… **the Lehman Crisis**　「リーマンショック」2008 年、アメリカ合衆国に本社がある世界有数の投資銀行であるリーマン・ブラザーズが破綻したことに端を発した世界的金融恐慌。

l. 19-20 … **the prefecture from which Kumamon derives his name**　「くまモンの名前の由来となっている県（＝熊本県）」A is derived from B「A は B に由来する」

l. 23 …… **those who ...**　「…な人々」those は people の意味。

l. 35-36 … **Kumamon is Kumamon, no strings attached**　先に蒲島知事がくまモンの成長戦略に挙げたシンプルなデザインをさらに詳しく説明したもの。つまり名前以外、熊本県らしいところがないくまモンは、くまモンでしかなく、くまモンを使用すると何か義務を負うような「ひも付き＝条件付き」（strings attached）ではないことを指している。

l. 48 …… **have room to do**　「…する余地がある」room は uncountable（数えられない名詞）で「余地、余裕」を意味する。

l. 55 …… **help O** 動詞の原型　（おさらい）「O が…するのを手伝う」原型が来ることに注意。

Checking Your Understanding: True or False

本文の内容に照らして合っているものにはTを、間違えているものにはFを書きなさい。

1. ___ Gov. Kabashima invented the mascot Kumamon to make people interested in Kumamoto and go sightseeing there.

2. ___ Most Japanese people recognize that Kumamon comes from Kumamoto at first glance.

3. ___ Gov. Kabashima encouraged the students to challenge new frontiers in their lives at the seminar.

4. ___ Harvard offered Kumamon a degree at the seminar.

How to Read a Paragraph

以下の問いに答えなさい。なお、(　) 内は正解が記述されている段落番号です。

1. くまモンの成功戦略である「シンプルなデザイン」によって、くまモンは他のマスコット（ゆるキャラ）とどのような差別化をはかっているのか説明しなさい。(Paragraph 4)

____

2. くまモンのもう一つの成功戦略である "no-fee" strategy ですが、企業に対してくまモンを無料で使用許可することで、どのような結果が得られましたか。(Paragraph 5)

____

3. 過度の露出からくまモンが飽きられることを心配した蒲島知事は、次にどんな戦略に出ましたか。(Paragraph 6)

____

Translating into English

Reading Passeges を見ずに、日本語に合うように（　　）内の語句を並び替えて、英文を完成させましょう。

1. リーマンショック後、私たちは価値観を経済から全体的な幸福に移行すべきだと私は実感した。
   After the Lehman Crisis, (overall / realized / shift / we / must / values / economy / I / to / from / that / happiness).

   ____

2. くまモンとは、熊本の観光事業の促進を独創的な方法で試みようと頑張っている知事の発明品である。
   Kumamon (promote / the / of / a / was / governor / eager / out / creative / ways / try / to / brainchild / to / tourism) in Kumamoto.

   ____

3. 最近の世論調査では日本人の 90%がくまモンを知っていると言っている。
   According to a recent poll, (they / of / people / 90 % / say / Kumamon / Japanese / recognize).

   ____

Listening Summary

下記の単語から正しいものを選んで空欄を埋めなさい。また、音声を聴いて答えを確認しましょう。

Kumamon, whose name is ①(　　　　　　) from Kumamoto Prefecture, where he serves as chief representative and promoter of the prefecture. Kumamon is the ②(　　　　　　) of Governor Kabashima, who was ③(　　　　　　) to explore new ways to ④(　　　　　　) tourism in Kumamoto. According to the Governor, the Kumamon character ⑤(　　　　　　) ⑥(　　　　　　) throughout Japan, as a result of a "no-fee" ⑦(　　　　　　) and its simple design.

• on • strategy • derived • brainchild • eager • caught • promote

UNIT

5 Saving Fukuoka's Street Food

福岡の屋台文化の歴史

© ペイレスイメージズ1 / PIXTA(ピクスタ)

1964 年東京オリンピックに向けて都市が浄化され（sanitized）屋台が路上から撤去された（removed）なか、福岡の屋台だけは当局（the authorities）と戦い続け、その屋台文化を守り続けてきた（preserve）。日本の屋台は第二次世界大戦（the World War II）中、現地の屋台に触れた中国や東南アジアからの引き揚げ者がそれを真似て（mimic）始めたものである。戦後（post-war）の食糧も職もない（unemployment）なか、手軽に店を持て、人々の空腹を満たすには屋台は最適だった。そんな歴史を持つ福岡の屋台文化も、現在では衰退（decline）の危機を迎えている。

Matching Words & Phrases

次の 1 ～ 10 の語句を、ⓐ ～ⓙの中の最も適切な意味と線で結びましょう。

1. aggressively	・	ⓐ 材料
2. reward	・	ⓑ 本物の、真正の
3. ingredient	・	ⓒ 礼を欠いている、不遜な
4. authentic	・	ⓓ （…が）ご褒美を与える〈with〉
5. prototype	・	ⓔ 陳情する
6. lobby	・	ⓕ 積極的に、精力的に
7. hygiene	・	ⓖ 衛生面
8. take over	・	ⓗ 先がけ、はしり、元祖
9. irreverent	・	ⓘ 引き継ぐ
10. spontaneous	・	ⓙ 気のむくままの、自然発生的な

Reading Passages

[1] While street food is enjoying a revival in the West thanks to the rise of gourmet food trucks, it's fighting to stay alive in Fukuoka, a city on Japan's Kyushu island.

[2] Although roadside food stalls, or *yatai*, have been a part of Japan's food culture for centuries, the period following the end of World War II saw a boom in their numbers. Japanese nationals returning to their homeland from China and Southeast Asia faced a struggling post-war economy and high unemployment, and many repatriates set up stalls mimicking the roadside eateries they had experienced overseas.

[3] Street food vendors were a common sight across Japan in the 1950s, but when Tokyo held the summer Olympics in 1964, many Japanese cities worried that the unregulated yatai might reflect badly on the image of the country's economic recovery. They took steps to remove them from their streets, and yatai all but disappeared from the country's north.

[4] It was a different story in the southern city of Fukuoka, however, where yatai vendors lobbied aggressively to continue their trade. Today, the city's oldest yatai have been operating for decades.

[5] Yatai menus offer a broad variety of foods, with individual stalls serving anything from tempura and grilled seafood to beef tongue; one yatai in Fukuoka even specializes in French provincial cuisine. In the Nakasu yatai area of Fukuoka's Hakata Ward, the specialty is the famous local ramen.

[6] Hakata is known as the home of Japan's *tonkotsu* ramen–a thick, rich broth made from pork bones and other ingredients simmered sometimes for days to produce a strongly umami soup with a powerful aroma. I've heard the pong of tonkotsu likened to dirty socks, wet dog and a steaming barnyard, but those who aren't put off by the smell are rewarded with a delicious and authentic noodle soup that has served as a prototype for ramen all over Japan. It's excellent served with *karashi takana*, the local spicy pickled mustard greens.

revival:「復活」
the West:「欧米」
see:「〈時代が〉〈事態が〉目撃する」
boom:「急速な増加」
national［名］:「（特に国外に住む）同国人」
unemployment:「失業（率）」
repatriate:「引揚者、復員者」
a common sight:「よく見られる光景」
unregulated:「規制されていない」
reflect badly on:「悪い印象を与える」
economic recovery:「経済復興」
take steps to ...:「…する措置を講じる」
remove A from B:「BからAを撤去する」
all but:「ほとんど」
trade:「商売」
individual［形］:「個々の」
serve:「食事を出す」
provincial cuisine:「田舎料理」
broth:「だし、スープ」
simmer:「ぐつぐつと煮込む」
umami:「うま味」
pong:「嫌な臭い」
those who ...:「…な人々」
put off:「食欲を失わせる」
pickled:「漬け物にした」
mustard greens:「からし菜」

7 More than the novelty or even the quality of the
40 food, which varies from stall to stall, it is the convivial atmosphere of yatai that makes them memorable. Fellow customers, often sporting a broad smile, are quick to welcome newcomers to a vacant seat at the counter, creating a casual and chatty camaraderie among strangers that is
45 unusual in reserved Japanese society.

8 The hospitality of the yatai operators also has its charms. Although not always the most inviting of hosts, yatai cooks, waiters and touts masterfully serve their customers from tiny mobile kitchens, battling against power outages, menu
50 restrictions and seething crowds.

9 Yet the vibrant culture of Fukuoka's yatai may soon be lost. The number of yatai in Fukuoka has been in steady decline for decades, from more than 450 in the 1960s to just 121 at the last official count in November. Popular with
55 locals and tourists alike, they face the same regulatory challenges as street food vendors everywhere, with authorities citing hygiene, food safety, waste management and occupational hazards as reasons for trying to control the operation and overall number of yatai on Fukuoka's streets.
60 What's more, a particularly unpopular local rule from 1994 requires yatai to close down once an operator retires unless a direct descendant takes over.

10 Another overhaul of Fukuoka's yatai regulations is slated for July, promising to increase the safety and quality of the
65 food while also providing mechanisms for new licenses. But while the goal is to preserve the city's yatai culture, it also runs the risk of sanitizing it.

11 One thing is certain: Fukuoka's yatai have always railed against attempts at regulation. Instead, they prefer to sit as
70 comfortable outlaws at the fringe of a bureaucracy that is enforced sporadically, if at all.

12 Fukuoka's food stalls belong to a dining phenomenon that is at its core irreverent, casual and spontaneous. Perhaps rather than saving the city's street food, the constant
75 attempts to regulate and control it may instead be hastening its demise.

novelty:「目新しさ」
convivial:「陽気な」
atmosphere:「雰囲気」
fellow customer:「常連客」
sport:「見せびらかす」
broad smile「満面の笑み」
chatty:「打ち解けた」
camaraderie:「仲間意識」
reserved:「堅苦しい」
hospitality:「おもてなし」
tout:「客引き」
power outage:「停電」
seethe:「ごった返す」
vibrant:「活気がある」
alike:「同様に」
regulatory challenge:「規制という難問」
cite:「…を引き合いに出す」
waste management:「廃棄物の管理」
occupational hazard:「職業上の危険」
what's more:「その上」
local rule:「条例」
direct descendant:「血縁の跡継ぎ、直系の子孫」
overhaul:「総点検、規制の見直し」
slate for:「…に予定されている」
mechanism:「方法、過程」
run the risk of ... ing:「…するリスクがある」
rail against:「抗議する」
outlaw:「無法者、やくざ者」
fringe:「周縁、はずれ、異端」
if at all:「仮にあったとしても、(この場合)取り締まるにしても」
hasten:「加速する」
demise:「消滅、終焉」

The Keys to Reading Passages

l. 1 ……… **the West** 文脈によって「西」の訳語は異なる。グローバルな文脈では「西洋」（反意語は the East「東洋」）や「欧米」になるし、ヨーロッパに限れば「西欧」になる。北米であれば「西部」になる。

l. 4 ……… **or** 「すなわち」の意味。A or B がここでは、A と B が異なるものではなく、イコールの意味になることに注意。roadside food stalls, or *yatai* など外国語の意味を表すときによく使われる。

l. 4 ……… **yatai** 「屋台」本文中の九州の yatai は伝統的な「屋台」を指すが、他にもトラックでの移動販売（gourmet food trucks）も含めて様々な形態の「屋台」を示す言葉が本文だけで、次のようなものがある。Ex. food stalls, roadside eateries, street food vendors, tiny mobile kitchens.

l. 6-8 …… **Japanese nationals returning to their homeland from China and Southeast Asia** 第二次大戦終戦直前・終戦直後、中国（満州も含めて）や東南アジアから日本（their homeland）に引き揚げてきた人々。あるいはそこで従軍していて復員してきた人々を指す。

l. 26-27 … **the Nakasu yatai area of Fukuoka' s Hakata Ward** 「福岡県博多区にある中洲の屋台街」那珂川と博多川に挟まれた約一キロほどの中州にある屋台街のこと。

l. 32 …… **umami** 「うま味」日本人の池田菊苗が 1908 年に発見した酸味・甘味・塩味・苦味に続く第五の基本味。だし昆布の中にグルタミン酸といううま味成分が含まれているのを発見したのが最初。欧米諸国には「うま味」に相当する語がなかったため、英語でもそのまま umami が使用されている。

l. 34 …… **a steaming barnyard** 「蒸している納屋（の周りの庭）」が直訳であるが、元々、barnyardy「（チーズが）納屋くさい」という単語があり、ここで並列された wet dogs とともにワインのテースティングで味・香りなど（特にイースト菌臭）を表現する決まった言い方。すなわち、dirty socks も wet dogs も steaming barnyard も強烈な臭いを連想させるものとして出てきている。

l. 52-53 … **be in steady decline** 「絶え間なく減少している」steady decline［形＋名］は名詞表現なので直訳すると「絶え間ない減少の状態にある」となるが、しばしば名詞表現を品詞転換して、動詞表現として訳すと日本語としてしっくりする場合がある。

l. 70-71 … **at the fringe of a bureaucracy that is enforced sporadically** at the fringe of a bureaucracy とは、直訳すれば「お役人たちの周縁に位置する」ことを表しているが、要するに「お役人に迎合せずに」いる様を言っている。また、sporadically は物事が「時々、散発的」に起こる時に使われる。ここではお上（役人）からの取り締まりが気の向いたときに行われることを表している。

Checking Your Understanding: True or False

本文の内容に照らして合っているものにはTを、間違えているものにはFを書きなさい。

1. ___ Except for the Southern city of Fukuoka, many Japanese cities sanitized yatai after the decision to host the 1964 Olympic games.

2. ___ The attraction of yatai in Hakata is the novelty and the quality of the food.

3. ___ The number of yatai in Fukuoka has been in steady decline for decades because the authorities have tried to control the operation.

4. ___ While, according to the authorities, the goal of regulations and control is to save the city's yatai culture, the author thinks that it may lead to the opposite result.

How to Read a Paragraph

以下の問いに答えなさい。なお、(　) 内は正解が記述されている段落番号です。

1. 第二次世界大戦終戦直後から1950年代にかけて屋台の数が急増した背景を説明しなさい。(Paragraph 2)

____

2. 1964年東京オリンピック開催にあたり、屋台の規制が厳しくなって、数が激減した理由を説明しなさい。(Paragraph 3)

____

3. Paragraph 10で書かれているように、当局が博多の屋台文化を守るべく規制の見直しを行うとありますが、著者はその結果どうなると予想していますか。(Paragraph 12)

____

Translating into English

Reading Passeges を見ずに、日本語に合うように（　　　）内の語句を並び替えて、英文を完成させましょう。冒頭に来る語でも頭文字を小文字にしてあります。

1. 海外にいたときに触れた道ばたの軽食屋を真似て、故国に引き揚げてきた日本人は屋台を始めた。

   (returning / set / homeland / stalls / to / their / nationals / Japanese / up) mimicking the roadside eateries they had experienced overseas.

   ____

2. しかしながら、（注：日本の）南部の都市、福岡では別の話である。そこでは屋台引きは彼らの商売を続けられるよう積極的に陳情を続けた。

   It was a different story in the southern city of Fukuoka, however, (aggressively / their / yatai / lobbied / to / where / trade / vendors / continue).

   ____

3. 取り締まるにしてもただ気まぐれに規制してくるお役人に迎合せず、むしろ気ままな無法者であるのを良しと彼らはする。

   (they / to / sit / outlaws / sporadically / prefer / comfortable / fringe / of / a / at / bureaucracy / as / that / is / the / enforced).

   ____

Listening Summary

下記の単語から正しいものを選んで空欄を埋めなさい。また、音声を聴いて答えを確認しましょう。

The history of Fukuoka's yatai culture has experienced ①(　　　　　　　　) fights against the ②(　　　　　　　　) who have tried to ③(　　　　　　　　) and control it. Especially when they decided to host the 1964 Olympic games, the authorities ④(　　　　　　　　) yatai from many cities and cleaned up the streets. Still, the Fukuoka city's yatai culture ⑤(　　　　　　　　) at that time. However, the number of the city's yatai has been in ⑥(　　　　　　　　) ⑦(　　　　　　　　).

• authorities • steady • decline • aggressive • removed • regulate • survived

UNIT

6 A Japanese Artist Finds New Life A Year After the Quake

ある芸術家の再生と「成長」

Missing in Action
1999年
acrylic on canvas
180.4 × 144.7 cm
© Yoshitomo Nara

2011年3月11日、東北地方を中心に大地震と津波が日本を襲った。東日本大震災発生から時が経過しても、福島原発の問題や遅々として進まぬ復興に多くの人が苛立つ一方、それまでの価値観の崩壊に苦しんだ人も多い。現代芸術家（a contemporary artist）奈良美智もその一人である。震災後、何も制作できなくなった（mired in a creative crisis）奈良氏は、母校（alma mater）に一種のアーティスト・イン・レジデンス（resident of sorts）として戻り、学生と共に半年を過ごす。そこで取り戻した芸術に対する信頼と新たな作風とは——。奈良氏の再生と「成長」の軌跡を追う。

Matching Words & Phrases

次の1～10の語句を、ⓐ～ⓙの中の最も適切な意味と線で結びましょう。

1. invent	・	ⓐ …を（想像力で）生み出す
2. enterprise	・	ⓑ（人が…するよう）せき立てる
3. superficial	・	ⓒ 表面
4. prove	・	ⓓ（要求・義務・主義などに）厳しい
5. strict	・	ⓔ（事・人が）とっぴな
6. spur O to do	・	ⓕ 企て
7. evoke	・	ⓖ（記憶・感情などを）喚起する
8. peer	・	ⓗ（真実なものでなく）見せかけの
9. surface	・	ⓘ（能力・資格などが）同等の人、匹敵する人
10. weird	・	ⓙ（…であることが）わかる

Reading Passages

[1] Yoshitomo Nara, one of Japan's top contemporary artists, spent much of last year mired in a creative crisis.

[2] The artist is internationally known for his wry, comic-style paintings of Japan's "latchkey" children, many of whom spend long evenings at home alone, inventing wacky ways to entertain themselves while their parents work late. Mr. Nara's works have always been characterized as graphically spare, the faces of his lonely, tough children outlined with thick brushstrokes so they appear mask-like.

[3] Yet after last year's deadly earthquake and tsunami in Japan–today marks the disaster's first anniversary–Mr. Nara said he was so heartsick he didn't want to make art at all anymore. The whole enterprise felt "superficial," he said.

[4] Mr. Nara lives an hour away from the earthquake's epicenter in Fukushima, so for months he avoided his studio and instead volunteered with quake-related relief groups.

[5] Then last fall it hit him: Perhaps he could creatively reboot if he went back to the studio where he started, the countryside classrooms of his alma mater, the Aichi Prefectural University of Fine Arts and Music. He asked the school's principal if he could come back, not as a teacher or even a student, but as a resident of sorts with studio privileges.

[6] The school agreed, and for the past six months, he's been sharing a studio with its students—working alongside them, even eating communal meals and helping them clean up afterward.

[7] The experience has proved transformative, he said. The students are "strict" but "pure" in their views on art, and his conversations with them have spurred him to experiment. He's started making 6 foot high clay sculptures of children's heads whose expressive features and rougher surfaces evoke Auguste Rodin of "The Thinker" more than the smooth, anime style of peers like Takashi Murakami.

[8] He's also started drawing portraits of girls whose facial expressions seem softer and more naturalistic than his past work, their cheeks feathered with Cy Twombly swirls and cross-hatching pencil marks.

wacky:「風変わりな」
be characterized as ...:「…が特徴と見なされている」
spare:「簡潔明瞭な」
outline:「輪郭を描く」
thick brushstrokes:「太い筆遣い」
deadly:「多くの命を奪った」
today:=2012年3月11日
disaster:「災害」
heartsick:「悲嘆にくれた」
epicenter:「震源地の真上にある地点」
quake-related relief groups:「被災者支援団体」
reboot:「再起動する」
communal meals:「同じ釜の飯」
transformative:「変化させる力がある」
foot:「フィート」= 30.480cm
clay sculpture:「粘土彫刻」
expressive:「表情に富む」
feature:「顔つき」
portrait:「肖像画」
naturalistic:「自然体な」
feather:[動]「羽のようにフサフサと覆う」
swirl:「うずまき」
cross-hatching:「(ペン画などで網目状に陰影を描く)クロスハッチング」

9 Mr. Nara said the nurturing environment did the trick–
40 the school's graduating class even gave him a faux diploma last month–and now he's getting ready to head back into his own studio again to paint. "It's weird to admit this because I'm already an adult, but I feel I've just grown up," he said.

10 So far, the art world seems to agree: Earlier this week,
45 Pace Gallery unveiled some of his new works on paper at a New York art fair called the Art Show, and every piece sold within the fair's first hour. The works were priced up to $50,000 apiece.

nurturing environment:「人を育てる環境」
do the trick:「目的を達成する、功を奏す」
faux:「偽の」= fake
diploma:「卒業証書」
unveil:「初公開する」
piece:「作品」
apiece:「一作品につき」

The Keys to Reading Passages

l. 4 ……… **"latchkey" children** 「鍵っ子」小学生が学校から帰宅する際、親が様々な事情から不在のため、自分で鍵を開けて自宅に入り親が帰宅するまで子供だけで過ごす子供のこと。

l. 11 …… **the disaster's first anniversary** 「東日本大震災の一周年」anniversary は毎年の記念日で、いい出来事にも不幸な出来事にも使う。Ex.「…周年、…回忌」

l. 17 …… **it hits 人 (that)** 「(考えなどが) 人に浮かぶ」この場合、コロン (:) 以下のことが奈良氏の頭に浮かんだ内容となる。同様の表現として "it occurs to 人 (that)" や "it strikes 人 (that)" がある。Ex. It never occurred to him that she should be angry.「彼女が怒るなんて彼は思いもしなかった。」なお、hit は不規則動詞で hit–hit (過去形) –hit (過去分詞形) と活用することにも注意。

l. 19-20 … **the Aichi Prefectural University of Fine Arts and Music** 「愛知県立芸術大学」1966 年設置の愛知県長久手市にある美術学部・音楽学部を擁した芸術大学。東京藝術大学、京都市立芸術大学、金沢美術工芸大学、沖縄県立芸術大学とともに年に一回、五芸祭を持ち回りで開催し、芸術文化活動の交流をはかっている。

l. 22-23 … **a resident of sorts with studio privileges** 「アトリエ使用の特権を付与された一種のレジデント」とは、「アーティスト・イン・レジデンス」(an artist in residence) の一種である。アーティスト・イン・レジデンスとは「芸術家の『滞在型の活動』を指すもので、欧米の大学や美術館、あるいはオーケストラ等で盛んに行われているものです。」(愛知県立芸術大学の公式 HP より) 愛知県立芸術大学ではアーティスト・イン・レジデンスの制度を設けて、以下のように紹介している。「日常的な活動の場を共有することで、より緊密な交流が可能となることがこのプログラムの大きな特徴でもあります。」(同 HP より)

l. 33 …… **Auguste Rodin of "The Thinker"** フランスの彫刻家オーギュスト・ロダン (1840-1917) の彫刻作品「考える人」。

l. 34 …… **Takashi Murakami** 村上隆 (1962-) は奈良美智と並んで世界的な評価を受けている現代芸術家。ポップ・カルチャーを援用した作風で知られている。

l. 37 …… **Cy Twombly** サイ・トゥオンブリー (1928-2011) はアメリカの画家。落書きのような線が特徴的な抽象画を描くことで知られている。

Checking Your Understanding: True or False

本文の内容に照らして合っているものにはTを、間違えているものにはFを書きなさい。

1. ___ Right after the 3.11 Earthquake, Mr. Nara felt as if everything were superficial and could do nothing creative.

2. ___ The Aichi Prefectural University of Fine Arts and Music invited Mr. Nara as a teacher.

3. ___ Mr. Nara's works used to be more similar to Rodin's than Takashi Murakami's.

4. ___ The art world highly appreciated Mr. Nara's experimental works inspired by the six-month stay with the students at the Aichi Prefectural University of Fine Arts and Music, his alma mater.

How to Read a Paragraph

以下の問いに答えなさい。なお、（ ）内は正解が記述されている段落番号です。

1. 東日本大震災前の奈良美智の作風はどのようなものでしたか。「鍵っ子」の子供の絵を例に説明しなさい。（Paragraph 2）

   ____

2. 東日本大震災後、母校の学生と共に過ごして奈良氏の作風はどのように変化しましたか。（Paragraph 8）

   ____

3. 奈良氏は6ヶ月、学生とともに過ごして、母校を去るときどのような感慨を得ましたか。（Paragraph 9）

   ____

Translating into English

Reading Passeges を見ずに、日本語に合うように（　　　）内の語句を並び替えて、英文を完成させましょう。

1. 日本を代表する現代芸術家の一人、奈良美智は、昨年のほとんど、創作の危機に陥っていた。
   Yoshitomo Nara, one of Japan's top contemporary artists, (year / much / in / creative / last / spent / mired / a / of / crisis).

   ____

2. おそらく彼がスタートを切ったアトリエに戻れば、創作的に再スタートを切れるのではないかと思った。
   Perhaps (back / could / started / studio / creatively / he / he / where / reboot / if / he / went / to / the).

   ____

3. 奈良氏は人を育てる環境が功を奏したと言った。
   Mr. Nara (trick / nurturing / the / did / the / environment / said).

   ____

Listening Summary

下記の単語から正しいものを選んで空欄を埋めなさい。また、音声を聴いて答えを確認しましょう。

After the deadly ①(　　　　　　　　) that had happened on the 11th of March, 2011, Mr. Nara experienced a serious ②(　　　　　　　　) in his creation. Then it ③(　　　　　　　　) him that he could creatively ④(　　　　　　　　) if he could go back to his ⑤(　　　　　　　　) environment. Therefore, he asked the school's principal to stay as a ⑥(　　　　　　　　) of sorts with studio ⑦(　　　　　　　　), which worked out well.

• hit • disaster • privileges • nurturing • resident • reboot • crisis

7 Fictional Japanese TV Banker Takes Double the Payback

ドラマ『半沢直樹』ヒットの要因

半沢直樹を演じた俳優の堺雅人さん © Kyodo News

主人公・半沢の決め台詞「倍返しだ！」（"Double the payback"）でおなじみの大ヒットドラマ『半沢直樹』は、元メガバンク勤務の池井戸潤の小説が原作なだけあって、「競争的序列社会である日本の銀行業界」（the competitive, hierarchical world of Japanese banking）が垣間見られる（give a peek into）と評判になった。中間管理職（middle manager）で融資課長（loan manager）の半沢、敵対する支店長（branch manager）、喰えない重役たち（upper management）、上司からのパワハラ（harassment）によって精神的に追い込まれる同僚（colleague）。こうした登場人物の持つリアリティだけではないヒットの要因を読み解こう。

Matching Words & Phrases

次の 1 ～ 10 の語句を、ⓐ～ⓙの中の最も適切な意味と線で結びましょう。

1. competitive ・	ⓐ …するように命じる ★公的に命令を下すとき使うことが多い。
2. conservative ・	ⓑ 保守的な ★伝統的なスタイルを好む人やものを指す。
3. capture ・	ⓒ（主語が）人に…を思い出させる
4. instruct ・	ⓓ 競争的な、競争率の高い
5. turn out to be ・	ⓔ …であることが判明する
6. conceal ・	ⓕ 隠す
7. remind ... of ~ ・	ⓖ ためらう
8. due to ・	ⓗ とりこにさせる
9. hesitate to ・	ⓘ 説明する ★絵や図を書き、分かりやすく説明するときに使う。
10. illustrate ・	ⓙ …のおかげで ★悪い意味で使うときは「…のせいで」でも可。

Reading Passages

1 There has been much talk about banking in Japan this summer–but not for the usual reasons like overseas acquisitions or global expansion. Rather, the talk has been more in the living room rather than the boardroom, focusing on a popular TV series about a courageous but fictional mid-level banker: "Hanzawa Naoki."

2 The hit series, named after the main character, gives a peek into the competitive, hierarchical world of banking. Based on the novels of Jun Ikeido, who worked at Mitsubishi Bank (now part of Bank of Tokyo-Mitsubishi UFJ) in the 1980s and '90s, the program focuses on a middle manager who challenges his boss and even financial regulators if he believes they are doing something wrong.

3 In the extremely conservative world of Japanese banking, such a character would stand out by a mile.

4 The program, which started airing in early July on Sunday nights, has become one of the most popular on TV, with viewership ratings of around 30%.

5 What captures so much attention is the main character, Naoki Hanzawa, a loan manager at the fictional Tokyo Central Bank. He doesn't hesitate to challenge upper management and people outside the bank, brandishing his trademark expression: "If your enemies hurt you, take double the payback."

6 Among the many challenges he faces are unreasonable demands from his boss, the branch manager. In one storyline, his boss instructs Hanzawa to make a contract for a ¥500 million loan to a local steel company.

7 But the steel company turns out to be using fraudulent accounting to conceal massive debts, and files for bankruptcy a few months later. That makes it nearly impossible to recover the loan.

8 The branch manager dumps all the blame on Hanzawa, even though it was the manager's own idea to make the loan.

9 Yet Hanzawa discovers the steel company's president is concealing assets in a hidden account. Moreover, the president has a secret relationship with the branch manager,

for …:for以下は「理由」を表す。
overseas acquisition:「海外での買収」
rather:(文頭で)「そうではなく」
mid-level:「中堅の」
such a character would stand out:「そんな人物がいれば目立つだろう」
air:[動]「(番組を)放送する」
brandish:「(勝ち誇って)振りかざす」
unreasonable:「理不尽な」
contract:「契約」
loan:「融資」
fraudulent acounting:「不正経理」
massive debts:「巨額の負債」
dump on ...:「…に押し付ける」
asset:「財産」

and the two have conspired to set Hanzawa up. In the spirit of fighting back, Hanzawa vows to recover the loan.

[10] The series is entertaining without being too serious, while illustrating various problems people can relate to in their own workplaces. One character has a nervous breakdown due to the tremendous pressure and harassment from his boss.

[11] The story also gives a glimpse of Japan's banking world, where only a handful of workers rise to the level of executive director. Most others leave in their 40s or 50s to join smaller units or business clients.

[12] Under such circumstances, Hanzawa's unorthodox behavior and attitude appeal to viewers who know such things could never exist in the real world.

[13] One real mid-level banker at a major Japanese bank told JRT he watches the program regularly and chats about it with colleagues on Monday mornings.

[14] "Some characters in the drama remind me of people at my bank," he said. "In that sense, (the program) is so real. Although if you act like Hanzawa, you would certainly get fired," he laughed.

[15] On the message board of the program's website, one viewer wrote, "This really gives me the courage to fight back, and I feel better about starting a new week."

[16] Hanzawa's signature expression, "take double the payback," is now showing up everywhere–in magazines, newspapers and conversations. Even a politician has used it.

[17] On a recent Sunday morning talk show, urging the government to proceed with a planned sales-tax increase, former defense agency head Gen Nakatani said, "If Japan delays the planned hike in the sales tax, we'll see double the payback in turmoil."

[18] As well, shops run by Tokyo Broadcasting System Television, the network that airs the program, sell "baigaeshi manju," a bun filled with bean jam and stamped with the phrase, "Double the Payback."

[19] According to local media, the buns sell out quickly each morning.

conspire to:「(共謀して)…しようと企む」
vow:「誓う」
have a nervous breakdown:「精神的に追いつめられる」
tremendous pressure:「凄まじい重圧」
leave:「辞める」
unorthodox:「型破りな」
chat about ...:「…について談笑する」
in that sense:「そういう意味で」
get fired:「解雇される」
urge:「強引に推し進める」
proceed with:「続行する」
sales-tax:「(日本の)消費税の」
hike in ...:「…の引き上げ」

The Keys to Reading Passages

l. 12 …… **financial regulators** 「財務監査人」金融庁から派遣されて銀行などに定期的に調査に入る。

l. 15 …… **would** 仮定法の would。if 節を伴わず、主語が仮定の意味を表す時がある。Ex. A wise man would not do it.「賢い人ならしないだろう」

l. 15 …… **stand out by a mile** stand out「目立つ、際立つ」に by mile「一マイル先から」がついて、文字通り、一マイル先でも目立っているのが分かることになるので、「圧倒的に目立つ」の意味になる。

l. 20 …… **manager** management は日本語にもなっているが、英語の場合、意味が異なるので辞書を引いて確認してみよう。

l. 25-26 … **Among the many challenges he faces are unreasonable demands ...** 主語が unreasonable demands であることに注意。強調のため、倒置が起きている。

l. 29-30 … **fraudulent accounting** 「不正経理」。fraudulent は fraud「詐欺」の形容詞形。ちなみに会計士は「accountant」、後に出てくる account は「銀行口座」（→ l. 37）。

l. 44 …… **tremendous** massive（→ l. 30）と同じく圧倒的な大きさを表す。

l. 71 …… **run** ここでは「経営する」の意味。多義語であるため、辞書を引いて色々な意味を確認しよう。

Checking Your Understanding: True or False

本文の内容に照らして合っているものには T を、間違えているものには F を書きなさい。

1. ___ In the extremely liberal world of Japanese banking, Hanzawa would be a hero and change unreasonable rules.

2. ___ Hanzawa decides to challenge his boss, a branch manager but not upper management.

3. ___ Hanazawa finally finds that the company's president has stolen and hidden a huge amount of money in his secret account.

4. ___ "Hanazawa Naoki" becomes popular because Hanzawa and other characters are real.

How to Read a Paragraph

以下の問いに答えなさい。なお、（　）内は正解が記述されている段落番号です。

1. 『半沢直樹』が大ヒットした原因として、主人公の痛快な「倍返し」のほかに、どのようなものが挙げられますか。(Paragraph 10)

2. 銀行の出世レースから外れた人はその後どうなりますか。(Paragraph 11)

3. ドラマと、現実の日本の銀行業界との違いはどのようなものだと述べられていますか。(Paragraph 14)

Translating into English

Reading Passeges を見ずに、日本語に合うように(　　　)内の語句を並び替えて、英文を完成させましょう。

1. ヒットしたこの連続ドラマは、競争が激しく、序列の厳しい銀行業界を垣間見させた。
   The hit series (into / the / a / competitive / peek / gives), (world / hierarchical / of / banking).

2. 彼が直面する多くの難問の中には、彼の上司である支店長からの理不尽な要求がある。
   Among (unreasonable / the / challenges / boss / he / faces / are / many / demands / from / his), the branch manager.

3. この連続ドラマは、人々が自分の職場と関係があると思えるような、あらゆる問題を描いている。

   The series (to / relate / people / workplace / own / can / in / problems / their / various / illustrates).

   ____

Listening Summary

下記の単語から正しいものを選んで空欄を埋めなさい。また、音声を聴いて答えを確認しましょう。

TV series "Hanzawa Naoki" is very real and ①(   ) some people of their ②(   ). However, Japanese Banking is a very ③(   ) hierarchical world, so if you say to your boss "if your enemies hurt you, take ④(   ) ⑤(   ) ⑥(   )," or you'll get ⑦(   ).

• conservative • double • fired • reminds • colleagues • the • payback

UNIT

8 As Sentiment Improves, Red Lipstick Back in Vogue

赤い口紅と景気の関係

赤い口紅はハリウッドの黄金時代（the golden age of Hollywood）の女優によく似合う。女性らしさを表現する赤い唇。しかし時代は現代。バブル（the bubble period）がはじけると明るい色味（bright colors）は影を潜め、ナチュラルメイク（natural makeup）にヌードカラー（nude colors）一辺倒になった。しかし最近、海外のファッションリーダーたち（trend setters）は赤い紅を引く。この現象のもう一人の立役者（a influential figure）は安倍総理だ。彼が口紅をするわけではない。が、景気への楽観的な気分（optimism）が高まると、赤のような派手な色（bold colors）は飛ぶように売れる。アベノミクス（Abenomics）が流行を盛り上げているわけだ。景気への気分（sentiment）と唇の色味（shades）の秘密の関係を探ってみよう。

Matching Words & Phrases

次の 1 ～ 10 の語句を、ⓐ ～ⓙの中の最も適切な意味と線で結びましょう。

1. exceed	・	ⓐ（目標値などを）上回る
2. employ	・	ⓑ 追い求める
3. latest	・	ⓒ 当初の
4. fuel	・	ⓓ 最新の
5. previous	・	ⓔ 消費
6. consumption	・	ⓕ ふさわしい、適切な
7. confidence	・	ⓖ 使用する
8. pursue	・	ⓗ 自信
9. initial	・	ⓘ（感情などを）あおる
10. appropriate	・	ⓙ（時間・順序が）前の、以前の

Reading Passages

1 Long known to prefer natural makeup over bright colors, Japanese women are suddenly taking a shine to red lipstick again.

2 According to Shiseido Co., sales of red lipsticks for its flagship brand for the autumn and winter season have so far exceeded its initial sales target by 180%.

3 Bringing back memories of the golden age of Hollywood, vivid shades of lipstick have been employed in recent times to great effect by trendsetters like Taylor Swift, Katy Perry and Lana Del Rey. While one shouldn't discount the impact that celebrities can have on Japanese fashion, the major cosmetics maker says that it's another influential figure driving the boom.

4 Shiseido attributes the latest trend to the reflationary economic policies of Prime Minister Shinzo Abe. While "Abenomics" has helped push up stocks and fuel a new sense of optimism toward the economy among the public, the premier himself is generally not thought of as leading the pack when it comes to fashion, even if the deputy prime minister does.

5 To understand how Abenomics and lipstick match up, it's important to keep in mind the previous trend toward natural, subdued colors over bold colors really took effect when the country's economic pessimism was at its worst.

6 "The main sellers for lipsticks in the 2000s were nude colors that were close to skin color," Shiseido spokesman Shotaro Nagai said. "Young people were previously in favor of lip gloss that had very little color instead of a colorful lipstick. Now color is back, particularly bold red lipsticks," he added.

7 Shiseido says it has found a correlation between lipstick colors and overall economic sentiment. When consumption was on the rise, brighter colors tended to be favored. Most notably, demand was strong in the 1950s when Japan was rebuilding itself after the Second World War and in the bubble period in the late 1980s.

8 In a survey conducted this year targeting women between the ages of 20 and 44, Shiseido found that those with a

take a shine to:「好きになる」
flagship:「看板の」
discount:「軽視する」
major:「大手の」
attribute A to B:「A(の原因)をBにあると考える」
push up:「つり上げる」
stock:「株(価)」
optimism:「楽観主義」
subdued:「地味な」
take effect:「(色彩などが)効果を発揮する」
pessimism:「悲観的な見方」
at one's worst:「…の最悪の状態で」
correlation:「相関関係」
on the rise:「上向きで」
notably:「顕著に」
demand:「需要」
survey:「世論調査」
those with ... :「…な人」

positive outlook toward Japanese society and the economy
40 tend to associate red lipstick with a forward-looking attitude, confidence, and a desire to pursue change.

9 And while there's a well-established correlation between fashion and the economic climate, it still seems slightly unbelievable that in Japan, where conservative formal and
45 informal dress codes play a major role, women are planning on changing what color of lipstick they wear based on how the economy is doing.

10 Based on a highly unscientific poll by JRT, bright red lipstick still isn't generally seen as something that's entirely
50 appropriate to wear in an office environment.

11 It appears that interest is limited to young, fashion-conscious hipsters and not your typical OL (Japanese shorthand for a female office worker).

12 "I would only wear natural colors in the office. But when
55 I go out and want to dress up, I wear red lipstick," Yuko Yamamoto, a 25 year-old office worker said while holding a fashion magazine in Tokyo.

outlook:「見通し、展望」
associate A with B:「AとBを関係づける」
well-established:「定着した」
economic climate:「景気」
dress codes:「オンとオフの区別がはっきりした服装規定」
play a ... role:「…の役割を果たす」
entirely:「まったく」
... -conscious:「…に敏感な」
hipster:「新しいもの好き」
shorthand for:「…を省略した表現」
would:「よく…する」
while holding a fashion… ☞p. 46の**Long known to**の文法解説

The Keys to Reading Passages

l. 1-3 …… **Long known to prefer ..., Japanese women are ... again.** 分詞構文の文章。従属節（譲歩を表す副詞節）である Although they (=Japanese women) are long known to prefer ... の部分を、接続詞 although、主語の they（＝主節の主語）、そして受け身を作る be 動詞を省略して分詞構文にした。ちなみに通常は従属節の動詞は ~ing にするが、受け身の場合には being を省略する。

l. 6 ……… **exceeded ... by 180%** 「180%の差で…を上回った」byは「差」を表す前置詞。Ex. win by one horse length「一馬身の差で勝つ」

l. 9 ……… **to great effect** to ... efect の…に色々なものが入る。to good effect「効果的で」、to no effect「何の効果もなく」。

l. 9-10 … **Taylor Swift, Katy Perry and Lana Del Rey** テイラー·スウィフト（1989- ）、ケイティ・ペリー（1984- ）、ラナ・デル・レイ（1986- ）。ともに皆、アメリカ合衆国のシンガー・ソングライターでファッション雑誌なども飾るセレブリティ。

l. 14-15 … **the reflationary economic policies** 「リフレ（ーション）経済政策、通貨再膨張政策」一方では失業を減らし国民の購買力を高め、他方ではデフレ（物価下降）を克服しつつも（急激ではなく）緩やかなインフレ（物価上昇）を達成しようとする政策のこと。

l. 16 …… **Abenomics** 第 2 次安倍晋三内閣（2012- ）で安倍総理が掲げた成長戦略を軸とする経済政策で、安倍と economics（経済学）を掛け合わせた造語。もともと、アメリカのレーガン元大統領（Ronald Reagan、任 1981-89）のとった自由主義経済政策が Reaganomics（レーガノミクス）と呼ばれていた。

l. 19 …… **When it comes to ...** 「…のことになれば、…のことに関しては」という意味。…の部分には名詞または動名詞（~ing）がくることに注意。Ex. When it comes to cooking, nobody knows more than Mr. Bunji.「料理のことになれば、文治さん以上に知っている人はいない。」

l. 19-20 … **even if the deputy prime minister does** 「たとえ副総理がそうだとしても」安倍内閣の麻生太郎副総理は「おしゃれな伊達男」と評判。黒のロングコートにボルサリーノ帽と水色のマフラーで決めた姿を、*Wall Street Journal* は「ギャング・スタイル」と評したことがある。

l. 26 …… **spokesman** 「広報担当」言語が無意識に男性中心に作られているのに異を唱えた Political Correctness（政治的正しさ、差別用語禁止）の流れで、spokesperson（Unit 10 ⇒ p. 57）という性別を特定しない言葉が使われることがある。また Unit 13（⇒ p. 75）では spokeswoman という語も登場する。

l. 48 …… **Based on a highly unscientific poll by JRT** unscientific とは一種のジョーク。JRT の記者が身の回りや普段感じている印象から語っているので、「科学的にはかなり信憑性が疑われる世論調査」と自虐的に言って笑いを誘っている。

Checking Your Understanding: True or False

本文の内容に照らして合っているものにはTを、間違えているものにはFを書きなさい。

1. ___ Apart from the impact of trendsetters such as Taylor Swift and other celebrities on Japanese fashion, we have another influential figure as to the revival of red lipstick.

2. ___ Prime Minister Shinzo Abe is generally thought of as leading the pack when it comes to economics.

3. ___ The demand for red lipstick was strong in the 1950s and in the late 1980s, both periods when economy declined.

4. ___ According to a highly scientific poll by JRT, bright colors and red lipstick don't seem to be in vogue yet in Japan.

How to Read a Paragraph

以下の問いに答えなさい。なお、（　）内は正解が記述されている段落番号です。

1. 1990年代、2000年代にリップグロスやヌードカラーの口紅が流行したことは、その当時の人々の経済に対するどのような見通しを反映していると言えますか。(Paragraph 5)

____

2. 株価上昇と景気に対する楽観的な気分をもたらしたアベノミクスとメークの色味について、その相関関係を右記の段落から推測して説明しなさい。(Paragraph 7)

____

3. 景気が上向いて派手な色味の口紅が流行したとしても、日本ではすぐに取り入れられないと言われているのはなぜですか。(Paragraph 9)

____

Translating into English

Reading Passeges を見ずに、日本語に合うように（　　）内の語句を並び替えて、英文を完成させましょう。

1. セレブが日本人のファッションに与え得る影響を軽視すべきではない。
   One shouldn't (the / can / impact / on / Japanese / that / discount / have / celebrities / fashion).

   ____

2. 総理自身は一般的にファッションに関して言えば、集団を牽引するとは考えられていない。
   The premier himself is generally (not / the / thought / as / leading / of / comes / pack / it / fashion / to / when).

   ____

3. 資生堂は、日本社会やその経済に対して明るい展望を持つ人々は赤い口紅と前向きな気持ちを関連づける傾向があることに気づいた。
   Shiseido found that those with a positive outlook toward Japanese society and the economy (lipstick / to / tend / forward-looking / associate / a / red / with / attitude).

   ____

Listening Summary

下記の単語から正しいものを選んで空欄を埋めなさい。また、音声を聴いて答えを確認しましょう。

Recently, bright lipstick has taken over natural color lipstick. The ①(　　　　　　　　) Shiseido's sales of red lipstick for its ②(　　　　　　　　) brand have so far ③(　　　　　　　　) its ④(　　　　　　　　) sales target ⑤(　　　　　　　　) 180%. Also, trendsetters such as Taylor Swift ⑥(　　　　　　　　) red lipstick. However, another most influential ⑦(　　　　　　　　) is Prime Minister Shinzo Abe. Long known to be a correlation between makeup colors and the economic climate, Abenomics is pushing up economic optimism now.

• exceeded • figure • initial • by • flagship • employed • latest

UNIT

9 Japan's Aging, Female Criminals?

女性受刑者の倍増と犯罪のグローバル化

Photo by Kazuyuki Nagano

刑務所（prison）でも特に女性受刑者（female inmates）の高齢化（aging）が進んでいる。ここ20年で女性受刑者の数は倍増し（double)、女性受刑者の65歳以上の割合（proportion）は男性受刑者のそれ（their male counterparts）を上回る。また、男女の受刑者では経歴（profile）の傾向が異なる。女性の場合は既婚者（married）、高学歴（better educated）、精神疾患発症（occurrence of mental illness）の割合も高い。高齢女性の初犯は窃盗（first-time theft offenders）が多く、交通犯罪（traffic offenses）を除けば、実に90％以上が窃盗（theft）であり、そのうち82％が万引き（shoplifting）である。今、刑務所で起こっている女性（高齢者）の増加、さらに犯罪のグローバル化（the globalization of crime）の実情も見てみよう。

Matching Words & Phrases

次の1～10の語句を、ⓐ～ⓙの中の最も適切な意味と線で結びましょう。

1. incarceration	・	ⓐ（ある観点から見た）事物の様相、面
2. suffer from ...	・	ⓑ …に加わる
3. perspective	・	ⓒ 投獄
4. account for	・	ⓓ（資料を）編集する、収集する
5. corresponding	・	ⓔ …に苦しむ
6. figure	・	ⓕ 数字
7. take part in	・	ⓖ（犯罪などを）犯す
8. compile	・	ⓗ（…に）相当する
9. commit	・	ⓘ（…の割合を）占める ★「説明する」という意もある。
10. reduce	・	ⓙ 減少させる

Reading Passages

[1] The latest white paper on crime in Japan shows trends that at first glance appear staggering: The number of female inmates has more than doubled in the last 20 years, while a larger proportion of those woman prisoners are over 65 than their male counterparts.

[2] While the overall prison population has continued to fall from 2006, the rise in incarcerations of women and the elderly has remained steady, the white paper shows.

[3] It also notes that female prisoners tend to have quite a different profile compared with male prisoners: they tend to be married, better educated and have a higher occurrence of mental illness.

[4] But before delving further into the report, here's a little perspective.

[5] The proportion of women prisoners, while rising, still account for just 9% of the entire prison population. That is a little higher than the corresponding figure of 7% in the United States, though overall rates of incarceration are much lower in Japan. The number of elderly female prisoners the justice ministry is sounding the alarm over is just 285, as of 2012, still an extremely small proportion of the population. The overall population of women over 65, according to the internal affairs ministry, was estimated to be 18.2 million as of September.

[6] The report shows that 12.8% of the female prison population is over 65 in 2012, compared with 8.5% of male prisoners.

[7] "Elderly female inmates tend to be first-time theft offenders," said a government official in the research department of the justice ministry who took part in compiling the report.

[8] Of the elderly women arrested for non-traffic offenses in 2012, over 90% were for theft, of which 82% were cases of shoplifting, the report showed.

[9] She's also more likely to suffer from mental illness than her male counterpart.

[10] "Female criminals appear to come from a background that's different from men," the official said, referring to the

white paper:「白書、報告書」
at first glance:「ひと目見てすぐに」
staggering:「信じがたい」
overall:「全体的な」
the elderly:「高齢者」
remain steady:「一定に保たれている」
note［動］:「強調する」
compared with ...:「… と比べて」
delve into ...:「…を深く掘り下げる」
the justice ministry:「法務省」
sound the alarm:「警鐘をならす」
estimate［動］:「推定する」
official［名］:「役人」
arrest ~ for ... :「~を…で逮捕する」
be likely to:「…である傾向がある」

tendency for male criminals to be single and uneducated.
40 "More study needs to be done on why this is the case."

11 The report also highlighted what it called the "globalization of crime"–namely, crimes committed by foreign nationals residing in Japan. While the government pats itself on the back for continuing to reduce the number of
45 crimes by foreigners, the Japanese media and authorities—as in South Korea–routinely overplay the role of foreigners in Japan's violent crime.

12 Data showed that foreign nationals arrested for non-traffic crimes accounted for 2.5% of Japan's total arrest
50 rate. But putting that number in context is, according to the justice ministry, nearly impossible. There are just over 2 million foreign residents in Japan, accounting for 1.59% of the entire population. However, there are no official estimates for the number of illegal aliens living under the
55 radar.

13 "Without having a clear idea of the total foreign population in Japan, it's not possible to compare their arrest rate with that of the general population," the official said.

namely:「すなわち」

pat oneself on the back:「自画自賛する」

routinely:「決まって」
overplay:「強調しすぎる」

entire population:「総人口」
illegal alien:「不法滞在者」
under the radar:「ノーマークの状況で」

The Keys to Reading Passages

l. 7-8 …… **the elderly**　elderly peopleのこと。the形容詞で“... people”を表す。The rich（= rich people）やthe poor（= poor people）などよく使われる。

l. 15 …… **while rising**　「上昇すると同時に」分詞構文の文章で、while risingの間にthe proportion of women prisoners isが省略されている。

l. 21 …… **as of**　「（…を基点として）それ以降は」の意味。例えば、時刻表やルールが改正されたときにいつを基点として改正が有効になるのか明記するときに使う。Ex. Consumption Tax is raised to 8% as of April 1, 2014.「消費税は2014年4月1日から8%に上がります。」

l. 23 …… **the Internal affairs ministry**　「総務省」正式にはMinistry of Internal Affairs and Communicationsで、2001年に自治省、郵政省、総務庁が統合されて総務省になった。

l. 33 …… **case**　（多義語）この場合、「（警察などが調査する）事件」を意味するが、他の主な意味もここでおさらいしておこう。「場合、実例」「事情、事実」「問題」「状態、状況」（→ l. 40）「主張」「症状、症例」。

l. 37 …… **criminal**　「犯罪者、犯人」。offenderは「（法律上の）違反者、犯罪者」。culpritは「刑事被告人、容疑者」。

l. 43 …… **reside**　同じ居住を表す動詞でもliveより形式ばっている。また、inhabit（住む、生息する）は動物の大群や民族などが主語となり集団の居住を表すのに使う。

l. 50 …… **context**　「（特定の事件などの）背景」Ex. argue in a different context「異なった事柄の背景で議論する」

Checking Your Understanding: True or False

本文の内容に照らして合っているものにはTを、間違えているものにはFを書きなさい。

1. ___ Elderly female prisoners tend to be married, educated and occasionally suffer from mental illness compared with young ones.

2. ___ Most male inmates suffer from mental illness.

3. ___ According to the report, the population of female inmates who were over 65 was 12.8% of all inmates in 2012.

4. ___ It is impossible to know the number of foreign nationals living in Japan.

How to Read a Paragraph

以下の問いに答えなさい。なお、（　）内は正解が記述されている段落番号です。

1. ここ 20 年で起こっている受刑者の傾向の変化を説明しなさい。（Paragraph 1）

____

2. 女性受刑者の経歴は男性受刑者の経歴の傾向とどのように異なりますか。（Paragraph 3）

____

3. なぜ日本に住む外国人の犯罪者の実数を把握することは不可能なのか説明しなさい。（Paragraph 12）

____

Translating into English

Reading Passeges を見ずに、日本語に合うように（　　　）内の語句を並び替えて、英文を完成させましょう。冒頭に来る語でも頭文字を小文字にしてあります。

1. 女性収監者の割合は、一方では上昇しつつあるが、いまだに全収監者数の 9% しか占めていない。
   The proportion of women prisoners, while rising, (population / account / for / just / of / entire / 9% / still / the / prison).

   ____

2. 2012 年に交通違反以外で逮捕された高齢女性のうち 90% 以上が窃盗罪であり、そのうちの 82%が万引き事件であった。
   (women / the / elderly / arrested / of / for / 2012 / non-traffic / offenses / in), over 90% were for theft, of (were / cases / of / which / 82% / shoplifting).

   ____

3. 白書はいわゆる「犯罪のグローバル化」と言われるもの、すなわち、日本に居住する外国人の犯した犯罪についても強調していた。

   The report also highlighted what it called the "globalization of crime"– (nationals / by / in / committed / residing / foreign / namely, / crimes / Japan).

   ____

Listening Summary

下記の単語から正しいものを選んで空欄を埋めなさい。また、音声を聴いて答えを確認しましょう。

According to the ①(　　　　　　　　) white paper on crime in Japan, the number of female ②(　　　　　　　　) has more than doubled in the ③(　　　　　　　　) 20 years. Although the entire population of prisoners has decreased from 2006, the incarceration of ④(　　　　　　　　) and the ⑤(　　　　　　　　) has continued to rise. The female prisoners are likely to have a different ⑥(　　　　　　　　) from their male ⑦(　　　　　　　　). They tend to be married, better educated and suffer from mental illness.

● **last** ● **latest** ● **counterparts** ● **profile** ● **elderly** ● **inmates** ● **women**

UNIT

10 Cult TV Travelogue Lets You Share Wednesday's Ride

『水曜どうでしょう』ロングヒットの秘密

©HTB / 協力 CREATIVE OFFICE CUE

北海道のローカル TV 局（local broadcaster）製作の旅バラエティ番組『水曜どうでしょう』（"How Do You Like Wednesday?"）がオンデマンド配信サービス（VOD services：video on demand services）で全国ネットの大ヒットドラマ『半沢直樹』やハリウッドの大ヒット映画（blockbusters）を破り、新記録（an all-time record）を樹立した。番組開始当初、藤村ディレクターの野望に反して（contrary to Mr. Fujimura's ambitions）、周囲は人気を博し成功を収める（widespread success）とは期待していなかった（had few expectations）。が、じわじわと人気が広がりローカルネットで全国区（nationwide）に躍り出た。従来の TV の常識（formula）を覆した鍵は、旅の目的が行き先（destination）ではないというところにありそうだ。

Matching Words & Phrases

次の 1 ～ 10 の語句を、ⓐ ～ⓙの中の最も適切な意味と線で結びましょう。

1. add up to ...	・	ⓐ 念頭にない、気づかない
2. annual	・	ⓑ 実際には
3. sales figure	・	ⓒ 合計…となる
4. break up	・	ⓓ 一年間の、その年の
5. feature	・	ⓔ …を大々的に扱う
6. purchased	・	ⓕ 購入された
7. strain	・	ⓖ （心身の）疲労
8. oblivious	・	ⓗ 商品
9. merchandise	・	ⓘ （関係などを）終わらせる
10. virtually	・	ⓙ 売上高

Reading Passages

1 "How Do You Like Wednesday?" strays far from the tired Japanese TV formula of a half-travel, half-food program. Instead the cult travel show is more like a road movie. Rather than beautiful locations or sizzling delicacies, the show mostly features the conversation of the presenters (and often their production crew). As for the destinations, they are sometimes chosen at random along with the mode of transportation–a recipe for unexpected results.

2 "The best part of a trip is not the moment when you arrive at the destination, but the strange things that happen along the way" said the program's director Tadahisa Fujimura, himself a fan of traveling.

3 The show features four middle-aged men: an actor, his boss and two program creatives. During its 17-year history, the team has traveled around many well-known tourist destinations in Japan, along with famous sightseeing spots in North America, Europe and Asia.

4 It started out in 1996 as a Hokkaido-only late-night program. Contrary to Mr. Fujimura's ambitions to make it popular nationwide, local TV station Hokkaido Television Broadcasting Co. had few expectations of any widespread success.

5 "I didn't want to create a typical locally produced show that just sends out virtually unknown entertainers to nearby locations," Mr. Fujimura said. "So I didn't give it a local feel. I wanted to make it popular. I wanted to be able to film the show overseas," Mr. Fujimura said.

6 Given the difficulties of landing a big name celebrity for a local TV station, Mr. Fujimura decided to pack the program with random elements instead. Shows typically start with main presenter Yo Oizumi supposedly captured by surprise on a home-use video camera, oblivious as to where he will be taken. The presenter was just a college student when the program started, but he is now an established actor.

7 The show quickly became popular by word of mouth, spreading to local broadcasters nationwide and achieving a peak rating of 18.6% in the program's home Sapporo region in 1999. With around 40% of connected TVs operating on

stray:「コースからそれる」
sizzling delicacies:「ジュージューとおいしそうな音を立てるごちそう」
presenter:「司会者」
production crew:「制作班」
mode of transportation:「移動手段」
recipe:「秘訣、こつ」
unexpected:「思いがけない」
middle-aged:「中高年の」
creative:「制作者」
Co. :companyの省略形
give ~ a ... feel:「~に…の感じを与える」
film[動]:「撮影する」
given [接]:「…と仮定すると」
land[動]:「獲得する」
supposedly:「おそらく」
capture:(ここでは)「…を撮影する」
by surprise:「不意打ちで」
established:「地位を確立した」
word of mouth:「口コミ」
peak:「最高の」

that particular night, the rating means almost half of active viewers were watching the program, according to Video Research Ltd.

8 While the airing of the show depends on local broadcasters, the program is also available through VOD services. According to Japan's longest-running TV on-demand provider Actvila Corp, last week's "How Do You Like Wednesday?" scored an all-time record sales high for the company. An Actvila spokesperson declined to provide the actual sales figure, but said the program "soared far above" their second most-purchased program. "Hanzawa Naoki" is also available on the service, which offers 65,000 programs ranging from drama series and large-scale documentaries to Hollywood blockbusters.

9 Further proof of the show's enduring popularity are the more than 3.5 million copies of previous series that have been shipped on DVD, and the 50,000 fans who attended an outside event of the show in Sapporo. Harder core fans even retrace the steps of the presenters, often showing off their program affiliation with car or motorbike stickers as they make their personal pilgrimages.

10 Mr. Fujimura said sales coming from the program and related merchandise add up to ¥2 billion every year, more than 10% of HTB's total annual income.

11 Fans of the program often say they love its sense of reassurance, though given the stresses and strains sometimes suffered by the presenters, that comforting response is something of a mystery.

12 A clinical psychologist who wrote a book on the show in 2012, said the answer lies in the sense of a shared experience: Viewers feel as if they are traveling with the four guys in the program.

13 "The way the show is put together breaks up the traditional viewer-creator relationship, giving viewers the impression that they themselves are also sitting in the car," said Reiji Sasaki, the book's author and an associate professor at the Graduate School of Human-Environment Studies at Kyushu University.

14 Dr. Sasaki said the waves of unexpected twists to each journey are another key part of the program.

active:「活動している」
longest-running:「長く続く」
provider:「ネットを通してサービスを提供する会社、プロバイダー」
decline to:「拒否する」
soar:「上回る」
rage from ... to ~:「…から~まで幅広く」
enduring:「長続きする」
hard core:「筋金入りの」
retrace:「たどる」
show off:「見せびらかす」
affiliation:「つながり」
make one's pilgrimage:「参詣する」
¥2 billion:「20億円」
HTB:「北海道テレビ放送」
income:「収益」
reassurance:「ほっとさせる」
comforting:「気分が安らぐ」
lie in ...:「(答えなどが)…にある」
put together:「構成する」
associate professor:「准教授」
twist:「思わぬ展開」

15 "Nowadays we are asked to come up with and follow a good plan for everything, but through the program fans can get the feeling that having no plan at all is also acceptable, a liberating feeling that offers a sense of relief," he added.
16 "The difficulty fans have explaining why the show is so entertaining is similar to the trouble people have explaining how much fun they had on holiday to other people who didn't go with them."

come up with:「(アイデアなどを)思いつく」
acceptable:「受け入れられる」
liberating:「解放感をもたらす」
a sense of relief:「安心感」

The Keys to Reading Passages

l. 3 ……… **road movie**　道中で次々に起こる出来事が物語の中心となる映画のジャンルの一つ。

l. 21 …… **few**　few と little の違いは、前者が Countable（数えられるもの）を修飾し、後者は Uncountable（数えられないもの）を修飾する。また few と a few の違いは前者が「少しもない」のに対して、後者は「少しはある」。(little と a little も同様)。

l. 38-39 … **With around 40% of connected TVs operating on that particular night**「その夜に視聴可能な TV の 40% のスイッチが入っており」

l. 69 …… **as if ...**　「まるで…であるかのような」as if 節の中は仮定法を用いるが、口語では直説法を用いることもある。Ex. ... I feel as if I were a bird.（仮定法）

l. 75-76 … **the Graduate School of Human-Environment Studies at Kyushu University**　「九州大学大学院人間環境学研究院」

Checking Your Understanding: True or False

本文の内容に照らして合っているものには T を、間違えているものには F を書きなさい。

1. ___ "How Do You Like Wednesday?" follows the traditional Japanese TV formula of a half-travel, half-food program.

2. ___ The show mostly features the moment when they arrive at their destination.

3. ___ Although Hokkaido Television Broadcasting Co. did not expect any nationwide success, the program director, Mr. Fujimura's ambitions came true.

4. ___ Because it was difficult to land a big name entertainer for the local TV station, Mr. Fujimura created the program packed with random elements.

How to Read a Paragraph

以下の問いに答えなさい。なお、（　）内は正解が記述されている段落番号です。

1. 番組が、1999年に北海道地区で最高視聴率18.6%を記録したことについて、実質的には視聴者の約50%近くが見ていたと言っていますが、どういうことなのか説明しなさい。(Paragraph 7)

____

2. 佐々木氏がこの段落で言っている番組の人気の理由を説明しなさい。(Paragraph 13)

____

3. 佐々木氏がこの段落で言っている番組の人気の理由を説明しなさい。(Paragraph 15)

____

Translating into English

Reading Passeges を見ずに、日本語に合うように（　　　）内の語句を並び替えて、英文を完成させましょう。冒頭に来る語でも頭文字を小文字にしてあります。

1. 番組は大抵おそらく不意にホームビデオで撮影されたと思われるメインの出演者、大泉洋の映像から始まるが、彼はどこへ連れて行かれるかは気づいていない。
   Shows typically with main presenter Yo Oizumi supposedly captured by surprise on a home-use video camera, (to / as / will / be / where / he / oblivious / taken).

____

2. 番組放送予定は地元の放送局次第だが、その番組はオンデマンド配信サービスを通してでもいつでも見ることができる。

   While the aring of the show (depends / broadcasters / local / the / on), the program (through / services / available / is / VOD / also).

   ____

3. 視聴者はまるで自分たちがその番組の中で 4 人の男達と一緒に旅をしているように感じている。

   (guys / feel / if / four / they / the / are / traveling / viewers / with / as) in the program.

   ____

Listening Summary

下記の単語から正しいものを選んで空欄を埋めなさい。また、音声を聴いて答えを確認しましょう。なお、冒頭に来る語でも頭文字を小文字にしてあります。

①(　　　　　　) to the program director's ②(　　　　　　) that it would be popular ③(　　　　　　), HTB had ④(　　　　　　) expectations. However, the popularity of "How Do You Like Wednesday?" quickly became widespread. ⑤(　　　　　　) to Dr. Sasaki, the program made you feel ⑥(　　　　　　) ⑦(　　　　　　) you sat with the presenters in the car.

• according • contrary • as • nationwide • ambitions • if • few

UNIT

11 Want to Cosplay? Then Lose That Sword

コスプレを安全に楽しむ方法

写真：ロイター／アフロ

コスプレ（cosplay：costume play の略）は今や kawaii 文化と並んで日本の文化輸出戦略クールジャパンの最重要コンテンツの一つだ。東京ゲームショー（the Tokyo Game Show）やコミケ（comiket：同人誌マンガを販売するコミックマーケットの略）のような大きなイベントには大勢が押し掛け (draw crowds)、それぞれがお気に入りのキャラクター（favorite characters）のコスプレを披露する。イベントの主催者たち（organizers）が決定した「すべき、すべからず」(Do's and Don'ts) を学んで、安心、安全にコスプレのイベントを楽しもう。

Matching Words & Phrases

次の 1 ～ 10 の語句を、ⓐ ～ⓙの中の最も適切な意味と線で結びましょう。

1. extinguish	・	ⓐ 区別がつかない、混同する
2. attract	・	ⓑ（情熱・希望などを）失わせる
3. confuse	・	ⓒ けがをする
4. queue	・	ⓓ（人を興味などで）引き寄せる
5. ensure	・	ⓔ …に夢中である
6. get hurt	・	ⓕ 決心する、決断する
7. at one's leisure	・	ⓖ 都合の良いときに、暇なときに
8. in place of	・	ⓗ …の代わりに
9. intent on [形]	・	ⓘ 確実に…するようにする
10. make up one's mind	・	ⓙ 列に並ぶ

Reading Passages

1 On your way to the Tokyo Game Show? Trying to decide which costume to wear? Wait! The organizers of Japan's biggest videogame industry meet have come up with a long list of do's and don'ts for cosplay fans attending the event.

2 Cosplay, short for costume play, has reached an art form in Japan. Events such as Comiket attracts hundreds of thousands of manga and anime fans intent on demonstrating their affiliations by dressing up like their favorite characters.

3 The Tokyo Game Show also draws crowds of gaming cosplayers, especially on the weekend. And with game plots becoming increasingly movie-like in complexity and scale, the cosplay possibilities are endless.

4 Decisions, decisions. Will you plunk for an easy-to-recognize character from a blockbuster game series such as Monster Hunter or Final Fantasy, or go retro with something from Skies of Arcadia?

5 But before you pack your demon-destroying sword or ultra-fast yo-yo to give that final authentic touch to your zany costume, consider these pointers below from the organizers of the Tokyo Game Show, who say they've seen everything.

6 Is it a reasonable set of guidelines to ensure no one gets hurt or confused by anyone's identity, or an overly long list likely to extinguish the fun from a harmless act of narcissism? Make up your own mind.

7 **DON'T**

- Don't dress in a uniform that could confuse you for police, firemen, Self-Defense Force members or security guards. Doctor's coats and nurse uniforms are also a no-no.

8 - Don't bring guns, swords, or chains—this includes model guns, air guns, or items with sharp edges. If you want to put pointy spikes on your helmet or armor, you're out of luck, too. Use foam or soft material in place of weapons, but note that the organizers prohibit you from swinging those bad boys around.

9 - If you want to dress up as a yo-yo champion, as in

on one's way to ...:「…へ行く途中」
videogame industry:「ビデオゲーム業界」
meet:[名]「大会」
an art form:「一つの芸術形態」
plot:「(物語などの)筋、構想」
increasingly:「ますます」
complexity:「複雑さ」
plunk for:「…を完全に支持する」
pack:「携帯する」
sword:「剣」
authentic:「本物の」
zany:「滑稽な」
pointer:「助言」
identity:「身分、素性、正体」
overly:「過度に」
Self-Defense Force:「自衛隊」
items with sharp edges:「鋭い刃のついたもの」
pointy :「先のとがった」
armor:「甲冑(かっちゅう)」
be out of luck:「ついていない」
foam:「発泡スチロール」
weapon:「武器、兵器」

Chosoku Spinner, think again. Skate boards, roller
40 skates and fresh vegetables are also out. All accessories, including horns and shoulder pads, must be shorter than 50 centimeters.

10 - Don't wear costumes that might block traffic—that includes full-body outfits shaped like a big stuffed
45 animal (or dragon—popular in the wake of "Puzzle and Dragons"), papier-mache costumes, or long skirts or mantles that drag on the floor.

block traffic:「交通(往来)を妨げる」
full-body outfit:「全身着ぐるみ」
stuffed animal:「ぬいぐるみ」
papier-mache costume:「張り子の衣装」
mantle:「マント」
drag:「引きずる」

11 **DO**

- Wear underwear and/or spats. The booth babes show
50 enough skin as it is. It helps to ask yourself how absolutely essential is it to show midriff, cleavage, or chest hair to make your costume authentic?

booth babe:「(展示会などの)キャンペーンガール」
as it is:「そのままに」
midriff:「上腹部」
cleavage:「(女性の)胸の谷間」

12 - Come early—way early. The cosplay dressing room will be open at 5 a.m. for those who queue, allowing
55 cosplayers to enjoy the show at their leisure.

The Keys to Reading Passages

l. 1 ……… **The Tokyo Game Show**　1996年から毎年開催されているコンピュータゲームを主力とした日本最大規模の展示会で、入場者はコスプレで来ることも認められている。

l. 7 ……… **hundreds of thousands of**　「何十万もの」hundreds of「何百もの」やthousands of「何千もの」の表現と同種のものであり、それぞれhundreds、thousandsと複数形になっていることに注意。cf. two hundred「200」数を表すとき、hundredは単数形。

l. 8 ……… **demonstrate**　ここでは「披露する」という意味だが、Unit 2（⇒p. 9）では略語「デモ（＝何かの主張を鮮明に表すために行う抗議運動）」の意味で使われていることに注意。

l. 16-17 … **Monster Hunter, Final Fantasy, Skies of Arcadia**　「モンスターハンター（通称モンハン）」、「ファイナルファンタジー」、「エターナルアルカディア（北米・欧州でのタイトルがSkies of Arcadia）」。ゲームソフトのシリーズ名。

l. 19 …… **give ... touch**「（仕上げに）…の感じを付け加える」

l. 25-26 … **a harmless act of narcissism**　「（勇者などのキャラクターに扮して）ナルシシズム（自己陶酔）を満たすための害のない行い」つまりコスプレを指している。

l. 28 …… **for**　「として（＝as）」の意味になる。この場合は、"confuse A for B" は「AをBとして勘違いした結果、AとBを混同する」という意味になる。

l. 36-37 … **prohibit A from B**　「AがBすることを禁止する」

l. 37 …… **bad boys**　文字通り「問題児」や「反逆児」を意味するが、もう一つ、主にアメリカで使用される用法として英英辞典に以下のような定義がある "something extremely impressive or effective."「ものすごく印象に残るもの、あるいは感銘を与えるもの」　ここで振り回す（swing ... around）ものは「剣」や「ハイパーヨーヨー」であり、筆者はすこし大げさに後者の意味でbad boyを使っていると思われる。Ex. Why don't we put this bad boy in our test machine?「このぶっ飛んだやつをテスト機にかけてみない？」

l. 39 …… **Chosoku Spinner**　『超速スピナー』橋口隆志によるマンガ作品。バンダイから発売されているハイパーヨーヨーをめぐって、小学生の少年達が熱いバトルを繰り広げる。

l. 45-46 … **"Puzzle and Dragons"**　通称「パズドラ」で知られるソーシャルゲーム。パズルロールプレイングゲーム（パズルRPG）で、基本無料で遊べるが有料課金アイテムを購入するとゲームを有利かつ簡単に進められる。

l. 49 …… **spats**　スパッツ。足の甲を覆う脚絆型のゲートル。特に19世紀末から20世紀初頭にかけて用いられた。

l. 53 …… **Come early — way early**　「早く来て、早く去る」このwayはawayのaが省略された副詞。「去って」という意味になる。

Checking Your Understanding: True or False

本文の内容に照らして合っているものにはTを、間違えているものにはFを書きなさい。

1. ___ The Tokyo Game Show is the fun meet only for gaming cosplayers.
2. ___ The organizers of the Tokyo game show established rules to enjoy your cosplay safely.
3. ___ Mascot cosplayers like Kumamon are OK because they have no weapons.
4. ___ To make your costume authentic, you can bring swords or put pointy spikes on your shoulder as long as they are made of foam or soft material.

How to Read a Paragraph

以下の問いに答えなさい。なお、( ) 内は正解が記述されている段落番号です。

1. 東京ゲームショーに大勢の人が押しかけるのはなぜですか。(Paragraph 3)

   ____

2. どういう職業の人々のコスプレが禁止されていますか。また、その理由を説明しなさい。(Paragraph 7)

   ____

3. 東京ゲームショーでは武器の持ち込みが禁止されています。その代わりどうすればいいか説明しなさい。(Paragraph 8)

   ____

Translating into English

Reading Passeges を見ずに、日本語に合うように（　　　）内の語句を並び替えて、英文を完成させましょう。冒頭に来る語でも頭文字を小文字にしてあります。

1. ビデオゲーム業界の大会の主催者たちは「すべき、すべからず」の長いリストをそのイベントに参加するコスプレファンのために考え出した。
   The organizers of videogame industry meet (with / do's / have / up / a / list / of / and / don'ts / come / long) for (attending / cosplay / the / fans / event).

   ____

2. それは誰もケガをしたり、身分を混同させたりしないようにするために妥当なガイドライン集なのだろうか。
   Is it (gets / one / to / set / of / or / guidelines / ensure / confused / no / hurt / reasonable / a) by anyone's identity?

   ____

3. そのコスプレの更衣室は行列する人のために朝の 5 時に開く予定だ。
   (cosplay / 5 / at / those / for / room / will / be / the / dressing / open / a.m. / who / queue).

   ____

Listening Summary

下記の単語から正しいものを選んで空欄を埋めなさい。また、音声を聴いて答えを確認しましょう。

Before trying to ①(　　　　　　　　　) which costume to wear, you should read and consider a long list of do's and don'ts which the ②(　　　　　　　　　) of the Tokyo Game Show have ③(　　　　　　　　　) up with. It is up to you whether you think the list is ④(　　　　　　　　　) to avoid getting ⑤(　　　　　　　　　) or confusing someone as a professional like army, security guards or doctors. Make ⑥(　　　　　　　　　) your own ⑦(　　　　　　　　　).

● mind ● up ● decide ● come ● reasonable ● organizers ● hurt

UNIT

12 Fukushima Watch: Who Wrote the New Anti-Nuke Novel?

反原発の新刊本を書いたのは誰？

官僚（bureaucrats）や原発村（the Nuclear Village）の間で話題になった小説がある。反原発小説（Anti-Nuke Novel）『原発ホワイトアウト』（"Reactor Whiteout"）は福島第一原発の悲惨な事故（the devastating accident at the Fukushima Daiichi power plant）の後、原発再稼働（the restart of reactors）を押し進めようとする政府や原発村の、内部の人間しか知り得ないこと（insider's knowledge）が克明に描かれている。ペンネーム（pseudonym）を使った著者の正体を探るゲーム（guessing game）が始まった。奇しくも出版時（its release）、まさに世論の大反対にも関わらず（despite considerable opposition from the public）、安倍政権が原発再稼働を進めようとしていた——。

Matching Words & Phrases

次の 1 ～ 10 の語句を、ⓐ ～ⓙの中の最も適切な意味と線で結びましょう。

1. resurgence	・	ⓐ 無謀な、向こう見ずな
2. reckless	・	ⓑ 内閣 ★英国では cabinet。
3. administration	・	ⓒ 復活、再起
4. indictment	・	ⓓ たくさんの
5. idiosyncratic	・	ⓔ 一部分
6. plenty of	・	ⓕ 憶測、推量
7. portion	・	ⓖ 度を超えた
8. excessive	・	ⓗ 特異な、特有な（= peculiar）
9. speculation	・	ⓘ 犯人
10. culprit	・	ⓙ 告発 ★「起訴」の意もあり。

1 A new fictional account that seeks to illustrate the resurgence of Japan's "Nuclear Village" following the devastating accident at the Fukushima Daiichi power plant is climbing fast on Japan's best seller lists, helped by a guessing game over the identity of its mysterious author who appears to have an insider's knowledge of the industry.

2 The book, "Genpatsu Whiteout," which means "Reactor Whiteout," is a story about a reckless rush to restart the nation's reactors shut down after the Fukushima disaster in March 2011. Its release comes as the administration of Prime Minister Shinzo Abe is pushing for the restart of reactors despite considerable opposition from the public.

3 The novel was written by an unknown author identified as Retsu Wakasugi, and is pitched with the subtitle "Another Reactor Explosion Is Inevitable: Indictment from An Elite Bureaucrat."

4 While the author's name is clearly a pseudonym, the book appears to come from a government insider with an abundance of idiosyncratic details into the customs and behaviors of the people who work in and around the nuclear industry.

5 Its story line involves utility companies collaborating with government officials and politicians to push for the restart of nuclear reactors, wielding powerful personal connections to fight off opposition from local leaders, activists and the media.

6 The fast-paced novel comes with plenty of suspense, sex and a few excessive surprises. But what makes it readable is the detail of the personal and professional lives of the people who reside in their small circuit of Japan's nuclear power universe.

7 One portion talks of how young bureaucrats at the Ministry of Economy, Trade and Industry, which oversees utilities, are allowed to sleep on "old-fashioned leather sofas" in the private offices of senior officials of certain levels—but not of others—after they work late at night. In another part, the No.2 official at the energy agency sees a top lawmaker, a friend for 30 years, to give him talking points on reactor

fictional:「小説の形をとった」
account:「(報告」
seek to ... :「…しようと努める」
illustrate:「説明する」
reactor:「原子炉」
rush to:「性急に行動する」
disaster:「(大規模な)災害」
push for:「(…するように)強く要求する」
identified as ... :「…と同一人物とされる」
pitch:「売り込む」
subtitle:「副題」
explosion:「爆発」
inevitable:「不可避な」
abundance of:「多数の」
collaborate with ... :「…と協力する」
wield:「(権力などを)行使する」
fight off:「撃退する」
activist:(特にここでは)「反原発活動家」
readable:「面白く読める」
reside in ... :「…に居住する、生息する」
circuit:「周辺」
oversee:「監督する」
allow 人 to do:「(人に)…するのを許す」
senior officials:「政府高官」
give ... talking points on~:「…に~についての助言を与える」

restarts before a press conference.

40 [8] They are in a café at Hotel Okura—described as a favorite hangout among politicians and elite bureaucrats despite, or because of, its antiquated atmosphere—where the lawmaker automatically orders his favorite dish, "Special Creamy Wagyu Beef Curry," a real item on the menu.

45 [9] The author's biography says Mr. Wakasugi is a graduate of the law department of the elite Tokyo University and currently working at an unidentified government ministry.

[10] Political and government circles are abuzz with speculation over who wrote the book. "Genpatsu Whiteout," 50 published by Kodansha on Sept. 11, is already ranked No.16 of all books on Amazon Japan's bestseller list. Large book stores in central Tokyo display the title prominently in their new arrivals section.

[11] "A search for the culprit is on," Taro Kono, a ruling-party 55 lawmaker, wrote in a Twitter post Tuesday. "Suspected: 'someone who is a senior official at the energy agency with considerable career experience but now with lots of free time maybe as a result of being sidelined.' "

[12] Mr. Kono should have some idea. One character in the 60 book, described as a "lone wolf of the conservative party" with an anti-nuclear stance, is very much like himself.

press conference:「記者会見」
hangout:「たまり場」
antiquated atmosphere:「古風な雰囲気」
biography:「経歴」
graduate:「卒業生」
the law department:「法学部」
currently:「現在は」
unidentified:「特定されていない」
circle:「(同一の利害・職業などの)仲間、社会」
be abuzz with:「(話題で)騒然としている」
display ... prominently:「目立つ場所に陳列する」
on[副]:「続いている」
ruling-party:「与党の」
post:「投稿欄」
be sidelined:「第一線を退かされる」
lone wolf:「一匹オオカミ」
conservative party:「保守政党」＊代表的なのは自由民主党
anti-nuclear stance:「反原発の立場」

The Keys to Reading Passages

l. 7 ……… **"Genpatsu, Whiteout"** 『原発ホワイトアウト』ペンネーム若杉冽なる人物が書いた2013年に出版された小説。本の帯には「現役キャリア官僚のリアル告発ノベル」と書かれている。この小説が書かれた背景には着々と進められる原発再稼働への動きがある。

l. 16 …… **a bureaucrat** Countable（数えられる名詞）の「官僚」cf. bureaucracy「（集合的に）官僚」

l. 22 …… **utility companies** 「（ガス・水道・電気などの）公益事業会社」ここでは原発を運営する「東京電力」などの電力会社を指す。

l. 32-33 … **the Ministry of Economy, Trade and Industry** 「経済産業省」

l. 37 …… **the energy agency** 通商産業省の外局である「資源エネルギー庁」を指している。同庁の公式HP記載の正式な英語標記はAgency for Natural Resources and Energy。

l. 37 …… **lawmaker** 「国会議員」国会が立法府（法律を制定する権利を有する機関）であることから。

l. 54 …… **Taro Kono** 河野太郎（1963- ）は日本の政治家。自由民主党所属の衆議院議員（任1996- ）。1999年11月に書かれた河野氏の国政報告紙「ごまめの歯ぎしり」第11号において既に日本の原子力政策を批判して、原発を順次、他のエネルギーシステムに置き換えて行く事を提案している。

l. 55 …… **suspect** 「疑う」ここでdoubtとの違いをおさらいしておこう。
Ex. I suspect that the current bureaucrat wrote this novel.「現役の官僚がこの小説を書いたのではないかと疑っている。」[= that 以下だと思っている]
Ex. I doubt that the current bureaucrat wrote this novel.「現役官僚がこの小説を書いたなんて疑わしい。」[= that 以下ではないと思っている]

Checking Your Understanding: True or False

本文の内容に照らして合っているものにはTを、間違えているものにはFを書きなさい。

1. ___ The book, *Genpatsu Whiteout* is a story about an anti-nuclear movement which fights against a reckless rush to restart the nation's reactors shut down after the Fukushima disaster.

2. ___ Although the author's name was a pen name and unidentified, many believed that it was written by a government bureaucrat or someone inside the nuclear industry because the author knew the details too well.

3. ___ The personal and private lives of those who belong to the nuclear village are well written, which makes the book readable.

4. ___ Some guess that Taro Kono wrote the book.

How to Read a Paragraph

以下の問いに答えなさい。なお、(　)内は正解が記述されている段落番号です。

1. 小説『原発ホワイトアウト』が出版された頃、現実の政治ではどのようなことが起こっていましたか。(Paragraph 2)

____

2. 小説のあらすじをまとめなさい。(Paragraph 5)

____

3. 小説の中でホテルオークラはどのような場所として描かれていますか。(Paragraph 8)

____

Translating into English

Reading Passeges を見ずに、日本語に合うように（　　　）内の語句を並び替えて、英文を完成させましょう。冒頭に来る語でも頭文字を小文字にしてあります。

1. 小説の形をとったある新しい報告が日本のベストセラーリストを急速に駆け上がっている。
   (lists / seller / account / a / fictional / climbing / is / on / fast / Japan's / best / new).

   ____

2. 政界と政府周辺の小さな社会は誰がこの本を書いたのかをめぐって憶測が飛び交い騒然としている。
   Political and government circles (the / speculation / who / over / with / abuzz / are / wrote / book).

   ____

3. 「犯人探しは続いている」、と河野太郎はツイッターの投稿欄に書いた。
   "(is / the / for / a / culprit / search / on)," Taro Kono, wrote in a Twitter post.

   ____

Listening Summary

下記の単語から正しいものを選んで空欄を埋めなさい。また、音声を聴いて答えを確認しましょう。

With the ①(　　　　　　　　) of Japan's "Nuclear Village," a ②(　　　　　　　　) novel *Genpatsu Whiteout* appeared in 2013. When it came out, Prime Minister, Mr. Abe was eager to ③(　　　　　　　　) for the ④(　　　　　　　　) of nuclear ⑤(　　　　　　　　) although a great number of people were opposed to it. The author is still ⑥(　　　　　　　　) and political and government circles are abuzz with speculation over who the ⑦(　　　　　　　　) is.

• fictional • unidentified • resurgence • culprit • push • reactors • restart

UNIT

13 For Some, Scented Fabric Softeners No Laughing Matter

柔軟剤の流行と弊害

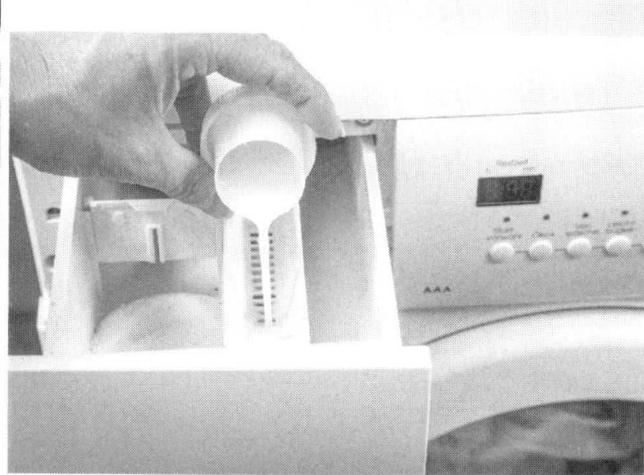

香りの強い（super-scented、fragrance-enhancing）柔軟剤（fabric softeners）の流行は、化学物質（chemical substance）に過敏な（hypersensitive）人たちにとっては生き地獄（a living hell）である。吐き気（nausea）や呼吸器の様々な問題（respiratory problems）、失神（blackouts）すら引き起こす。ある人は外出時には必ず工業用ガスマスクを着ける（wear a gas mask designed for industrial workers）。また香料を使用した製品の被害を訴えるある団体は、柔軟剤を疫病（pestilence）や公害（industrial pollution）などにたとえる。一方、消費者はしばらくすると（after a while）強い香りになれてゆき、必然的により強い香りを求めるようになる。このトレンドの行方は ── 。

Matching Words & Phrases

次の 1 ～ 10 の語句を、ⓐ ～ⓙの中の最も適切な意味と線で結びましょう。

1. humid	・	ⓐ 強力な（= powerful）
2. property	・	ⓑ〈名〉誘因、〈動〉誘発する
3. inhale	・	ⓒ（規則や信念を）忠実に守る
4. potent	・	ⓓ（多義語）効能、特性 ★「財産」「不動産」「所有」の意もあり。
5. be exposed to	・	ⓔ（においなどを）放つ
6. emit	・	ⓕ 湿度の高い、むしむしする
7. symptom	・	ⓖ 呼び掛ける、訴える
8. call on	・	ⓗ 症状、症候
9. trigger	・	ⓘ（肺まで）吸い込む
10. adhere to	・	ⓙ …にさらされる

Reading Passages

1 For Yuko Ozawa, the growing use of super-scented fabric softeners has turned life into a living hell.

2 Attracted by the smell of freshly laundered clothes, more Japanese are using fabric softeners with ultra-powerful fragrances. Softeners that continuously release scent for up to a month are a godsend for those fighting the musty smells of clothes stored in the humid summer. Others cite the therapeutic properties of a scented handkerchief, which can provide a pick-up during a dull meeting. In the six months to September, sales of fragrance-enhancing fabric softeners more than doubled in Japan, led by brands such as Procter and Gamble Co.'s Downy, and Lion Corp.'s Soflan Aroma Rich.

3 But for people like Ms. Ozawa, who suffers nausea, respiratory problems, and even blackouts when she inhales artificial fragrances, the potent scents coming from clotheslines have turned neighborhoods into minefields. Other triggers include scents from shampoos, cosmetics, and perfumes. Whenever she goes outdoors, she wears a gas mask designed for industrial workers exposed to toxic fumes.

4 "Little children look at me and cry or stare," said the retired teacher in her home in Gifu city, central Japan. Outside her door, signs warn visitors she may need to close the door on them if they emit too strong a fragrance.

5 Ms. Ozawa is one of a rising number of people reporting nausea and other symptoms from the growing use of fabric softeners. In the year that ended in March, the National Consumer Affairs Center fielded 41 calls from people who complained that the smell of fabric softeners made them feel ill. In the six months since April, the number has already passed 50.

6 "Concerts, plays, speeches, hotels, department stores, buses, trains—all these places where people come together are closed to me now," she said.

7 Dubbed "hypersensitive," people like Ms. Ozawa are campaigning for greater awareness of their condition. She has succeeded in having Gifu put signs up around city hall

freshly ...:「…したての」
launder:「洗濯する」
godsend:「天の恵み」
musty:「カビくさい」
cite:「(記憶を)喚起させる」
therapeutic:「癒し効果」
pick-up:「刺激」
dull:「退屈な」
minefield:「地雷原、危険が潜む状態」
toxic fume:「有毒ガス」
retired:「退職した」
warn:「警告する」
field[動]:「(電話·質問などを)てきぱき処理する」
complain:「苦情を言う」
dub:「(人をあだ名で)呼ぶ」
campaign for:「運動を起こす」
put ... up:「…を掲げる」

calling on people to limit their fragrance use.

40 [8] "Please Show Restraint In Your Use Of Fragrances. Fragrances can trigger allergic reactions and asthma attacks for people who suffer allergies or are hypersensitive to chemical substances," a poster reads. A handful of other cities have followed suit.

45 [9] The cause of sufferers of allergic reactions to chemical fragrances has been championed by other groups that take umbrage with strong scents arising from fabric softeners, including the Tokyo Anti-Pesticide Group. In letters to officials, such groups compare fabric softeners to "pestilence," 50 "industrial pollution" and "harassment."

[10] A spokeswoman at P&G's Tokyo office declined to comment on the matter, as did one for Lion, which attaches notices to products urging users to adhere to recommended amounts. A spokeswoman for the Japan Soap and Detergent 55 Association said it may ask manufacturers to recommend lower amounts of fabric softener per load.

[11] But consumer demand could mean fragrances only get stronger, according to Chuo Bussan International Co. (CBIC), which distributes Downy in Japan.

60 [12] "After a while, your nose gets used to fragrance," said Kayne Goodwin, brand manager of CBIC's marketing department.

[13] The Downy product lineup in Japan includes "Ultra Downy Infusions" fabric softener sheets that are tossed into 65 the dryer with clothing, and which contain a blend of scents such as jasmine or orange, and scent microcapsules called "Downy Unstoppables." CBIC suggests Downy sheets be placed into drawers, shoe boxes and cars, and that Downy Unstoppables be mixed and matched to create personalized 70 fragrances.

[14] "Users look for new fragrances. This trend will grow," Mr. Goodwin said.

limit:「制限する」
restraint:「自制」
allergic reaction:「アレルギー反応」
asthma attack:「ぜんそく発作」
a handful of ... :「少数の…」
suit:「要請」
be championed by:「支持する」
take umbrage:「不快に思う」
arise:「生じる」
compare A to B:「AをBにたとえる」
spokeswoman:「広報担当者」
notice:「通告、警告」
urge 人 to do:「(強く)…することを(人に)促す」
detergent:「合成洗剤」
manufacturer:「メーカー」
distribute:「(商品を)流通させる」
get (be) used to ... (...ing):「…(すること)に慣れる」
infusion:「注入」
drawer:「引き出し、たんす」
personalized:「個人の好みにあわせた」

The Keys to Reading Passages

l. 6-7 ……**those fighting the musty smells ... summer.** those = people。those who ... の形でもよく使われる。

l. 6 ………**smell** 「匂い、臭い」匂いに関する単語は他に次のようなものがある。scent は「好ましいほのかな香り」。fragrance は「かぐわしさ、香気」など香水などの甘い（一般的には）好ましい香りの意味になる。aroma も fragrance とほぼ同じで、香料などの香りも含む。smell は形容詞をともなって好ましい意味でも使われるが、単独で使われるとき「臭気」を指すのが通常。odor は匂いの発生源に重点を置く。

l. 11 ……**Procter and Gamble Co. = P&G** 洗剤などを手がける米国の会社。

l. 28-29 …**The National Consumer Affairs Center** 「国民生活センター」消費者保護を目的として設立された独立行政法人。直接、苦情処理を行うほか、消費者問題について調査研究と情報収集を行う。

l. 36-37 …**Dubbed "hypersensitive," people like Ms. Ozawa are campaigning for ... condition.** 分詞構文。"Dubbed 'hypersensitive,' " の部分は従属節（副詞節）で接続詞と主語、be 動詞が省略されている。すなわち、元の形は "As they (=people like Ms. Ozawa) are dubbed 'hypersensitive,' people like Ms. Ozawa..." である。

l. 38 ……**succeed in** in のあとに名詞あるいは動名詞（~ing）を伴って「…に成功する」という意味になる。併せて、succeed には「継ぐ」という意味もあることを覚えておこう。その場合は succeed to ＋名詞（…の後を継ぐ）になる。Ex. Her daughter succeeded to her property.（娘が彼女の財産を相続した。）

l. 48 ……**The Tokyo Anti-Pesticide Group** 「反農薬東京グループ」但し、グループの HP 記載の英語標記は No-Pesticides Action Network in Tokyo (NPANT) となっている。2013 年 6 月に環境大臣らに「香り付き柔軟剤の使用の推奨」を撤回することを求めた文書を送っている。

l. 56 ……**per load** load は多義語で基本的な意味は「重さ、荷重」だが、ここでは「洗濯物（一回分）」の意味。例えば、柔軟剤の注意書きには次のような指示が書かれている。Ex. Measure the softener to the fill line outlined in the cap for small, medium, or large loads.「洗濯物の量［少・普・多］に合わせて、キャップに引いてある線に従って柔軟剤を計量してください。」

l. 67 ……**Downy Unstoppables** unstoppable は文字通り、「止められない」という意味で、ダウニーの匂いが「どこまでもいつまでも（止められないほど）漂って行くこと」を暗示する。香りが強化された商品と思われる。

l. 67 ……**suggest (that) S (should)** 動詞の原型 「（考えなどを人に）提案する」「提案・命令・必要」を表す動詞は、見出しのような語形を用いることがある。should は省略可能で本文のよう S be など動詞の原型が主語の後にすぐ来る場合がある。

Checking Your Understanding: True or False

本文の内容に照らして合っているものにはTを、間違えているものにはFを書きなさい。

1. ___ Everybody is happy with enhanced-fragrance fabric softeners because they get rid of the musty smells of clothes stored in summer.

2. ___ Super-scented fabric softeners might cause serious health problems.

3. ___ Many other cities followed Gifu city and asked people to limit their use of fragrances.

4. ___ According to Mr. Goodwin, the more consumers use ultra-powerful fragrant fabric softeners, the stronger scent they demand.

How to Read a Paragraph

以下の問いに答えなさい。なお、( ) 内は正解が記述されている段落番号です。

1. なぜオザワさんは外出時にガスマスクを着用しているのですか。(Paragraph 3)

____

2. 日本石鹸洗剤工業会（The Japan Soap and Detergent Association）は香り付きの柔軟剤が健康被害を引き起こすという訴えに対して、どのような対策を講じると言っていますか。説明しなさい。(Paragraph 10)

____

3. ダウニーの日本販売代理店によれば、消費者のニーズはどのような方向へ向かうと述べていますか。その理由と共に説明しなさい。(Paragraph 11&12)

____

Translating into English

Reading Passeges を見ずに、日本語に合うように（　　　）内の語句を並び替えて、英文を完成させましょう。冒頭に来る語でも頭文字を小文字にしてあります。

1. 最長で一ヶ月香りを放ち続ける柔軟剤は、服のカビくさい匂いと格闘する人々にとっては天の恵みである。

   Softeners that continuously release scent for up to a month are (fighting / of / smells / those / a / the / godsend / musty / for / clothes).

   ____

2. 彼らは自分たちの状況にもっと気づいてもらおうと（促す）運動をしている。

   (campaigning / their / awareness / they / are / condition / for / greater / of).

   ____

3. 彼女は岐阜市に香料製品の使用を制限するよう呼びかける看板を市役所近隣に掲げてもらうことに成功した。

   She has succeeded (calling / signs / put / up / hall / in / around / having / city / Gifu / on / people) to limit their fragrance use.

   ____

Listening Summary

下記の単語から正しいものを選んで空欄を埋めなさい。また、音声を聴いて答えを確認しましょう。

The use of ①(　　　　　　　　)-fragrance fabric softeners has been growing in Japan, ②(　　　　　　　　) it causes various ③(　　　　　　　　) such as nausea for those who are ④(　　　　　　　　) to chemical products. Ms. Ozawa, one of them, succeeded ⑤(　　　　　　　　) ⑥(　　　　　　　　) Gifu city take some action. However, the trend of people's usage of super-scented fabric softeners seems ⑦(　　　　　　　　).

• **symptoms** • **having** • **enhanced** • **in** • **hypersensitive** • **unstoppable** • **while**

UNIT

14 The 1964 Tokyo Olympics: A Turning Point for Japan

オリンピックに見る日本のターニングポイント

東京 2020 オリンピック・パラリンピック招致 "Cool Tokyo" アンバサダーとしてプレゼンする滝川クリステルさん © AFP ＝時事

2020 年東京オリンピック開催決定直前に書かれた記事を読んでみよう。遡ること約半世紀、1964 年アジアで初めての東京オリンピックが開催された。招致決定が 1959 年、敗戦からわずか 14 年のことであったのだから、日本にとって極めて重要な（hugely significant）出来事だったことがわかるだろう。これをきっかけに日本は、平和で経済的にも自信に満ちた国として（as a peaceful, economically confident nation）国際社会の舞台に返り咲き（returned to the global stage）、国内では当時の国家予算に相当する額（the equivalent of its national budget）がオリンピック事業に投入され、都市の基盤（the city's infrastructure）が整備された。2020 年を仰ぎ見つつ、1964 年東京オリンピックによってもたらされた日本の変容を振り返ろう。

Matching Words & Phrases

次の 1 ～ 10 の語句を、ⓐ～ⓙの中の最も適切な意味と線で結びましょう。

1. legacy	・	ⓐ（比喩的に）燃え立たせる、あおる
2. emerge	・	ⓑ 遺産
3. devastate	・	ⓒ 統計
4. coincide with	・	ⓓ（…と）同時に起こるようにする
5. numerous	・	ⓔ 非常に多くの
6. renovate	・	ⓕ 破壊する、壊滅させる
7. temporary	・	ⓖ 一時的な、その時だけの
8. current	・	ⓗ 改修する
9. fuel	・	ⓘ 現在の
10. statistics	・	ⓙ（逆境などから）浮かび上がる

Reading Passages

1 Hosting the 1964 Olympic Games was hugely significant for Japan as it returned to the global stage as a peaceful, economically confident nation. It was also a massive undertaking, with some estimates suggesting Tokyo spent the equivalent of its national budget on a major building program that transformed the city's infrastructure–a far cry from plans for a slimmed-down 2020 summer games.

2 In a speech last month to support Tokyo's 2020 Olympics bid, Prime Minister Shinzo Abe described how the nation was still recovering from World War II when it won the right to host the 1964 games.

3 "Tokyo was chosen to host the 1964 Olympics in 1959, just 14 years after the end of the war. We were much poorer then than we are today," Mr. Abe said, rallying the crowd. "But Japanese back then were passionate about hosting the Olympics in Tokyo, and that passion fueled the success of the games."

4 Mr. Abe also has a personal connection to the '64 games. The prime minister at the time was his grandfather, Nobusuke Kishi. Like Mr. Kishi, Mr. Abe hopes staging the event will have a positive economic impact, adding momentum to an economy finally showing signs of emerging from decades of deflation.

5 The 1964 Olympics were the first held in Japan and in Asia, although Tokyo had won the right to host the 1940 Olympics. They were cancelled due to the outbreak of World War II and threats of boycott over Japan's military incursions into China. The games didn't resume until the 1948 London Olympics, by which time Japan had lost the war and been occupied by the Allied Powers led by the United States.

6 To symbolize Japan's recovery from the war, the Olympic torch was carried by Yoshinori Sakai, born in Hiroshima on Aug. 6, 1945, the day the atomic bomb devastated the city.

7 Among the many infrastructure projects timed to coincide with the event was the Shinkansen bullet train. The service between Osaka and Tokyo began nine days before the games kicked off Oct. 10, a date that is now a national holiday.

massive:「大規模な」
undertaking:「事業」
transform:「…を変容させる」
be a far cry from ...:「…と大いに異なる」
slimmed-down:「削減」
win the right to:「…する権利を勝ち取る」
host:「主催する」
rally:「…を元気づける」
passionate:「情熱的な」
stage[動]:「開催する」
add momentum to ...:「…にはずみを加える」
decade:「10年間」
due to:「…のせいで」
outbreak:「勃発」
boycott:「ボイコット、排訴運動」
resume:「再開する」
symbolize:「…の象徴となる」
torch:「聖火」
time ... to do:「…を~するように調整する」
bullet train:「新幹線」
service :「運行」
kick off:「(イベントなどが)始まる」

Haneda Airport was modernized and numerous highways,
40 expressways and subway lines built.

8 The Japan Olympic Committee says 30 venues were used in the 1964 games, including new, renovated and temporary ones, in Tokyo and four other prefectures. Some of these, including Yoyogi National Gymnasium, where the swimming
45 and basketball events were held, will be used again if Tokyo beats rivals Madrid and Istanbul in Saturday's ballot in Buenos Aires.

9 That would help make a 2020 games among the cheapest in recent times, undercutting Beijing ($40 billion), London
50 ($14 billion) and the estimated cost ($14.4 billion) of the Rio de Janeiro games, according to ratings agency Standard and Poor's. The estimated costs of the 2020 Games would be ¥773 billion ($7.7 billion), less than 1% of the national budget. S&P estimates the central and metropolitan
55 governments spent more than $3 billion based on the exchange rate of the time to host the 1964 games, or about $10 billion at the current rate, roughly equivalent to the entire national budget that year.

10 The 1964 games were a great sporting success for Japan.
60 The nation had a delegation of 437 officials and athletes, and won 16 gold medals, five silver and eight bronze, coming in third in the medal total behind the United States and the Soviet Union. It won five golds each in wrestling and men's gymnastics. The women's volleyball team won gold after
65 beating the Soviets in the final.

11 The games had memorable champions too, including Abebe Bikila of Ethiopia, the first athlete to win the marathon twice, and Soviet gymnast Larysa Latynina, who brought her career medal total to 18.

70 12 A growing middle class rushed to buy television sets to watch the games, as well as other household appliances, leading to the term "Olympic economy." The games were broadcast to the world using communication satellites. It was the first Olympics to use computers to keep statistics.

75 13 And in an effort to "beautify" the city, Tokyo promoted hygiene, cleaning its streets and rivers and planting greenery–a legacy that lives on in the city.

modernize:「近代化する」
highway:「幹線道路」
expressway:「高速道路」
committee:「委員会」
venue:「会場」
be held:「(大会などを)開催する」
beat ...:「…を負かす」
ballot:「投票」
undercut:「削減する」
ratings agency:「格付け機関」
the metropolitan government:「東京都政」
exchange rate:「為替相場」
delegation:「代表選手団」
official:「競技役員」
come in ...:「…位になる」
wrestling:「レスリング」
gymnastics:「体操競技」
final[名]:「決勝戦」
memorable:「忘れられない」
career:「経歴(選手生活)」
as well as ...:「…と同様に」
household appliance:「家庭用電化製品」
lead to ...:「…を生み出す」
term:「表現」
broadcast[動]:「放送する」
communication satellites:「通信衛生、CS」
in an effort to do:「…しようとして」
promote:「促進する」
greenery:「緑樹」

The Keys to Reading Passages

l. 9 ……… **bid** 「入札」が元々の意味であるが、この場合、オリンピック招致に「立候補すること」を指している。

l. 10 …… **recover from** 「回復する」が基本の意味だが、文脈に応じて何から回復するのか考える必要がある。この場合、戦争の後の「回復」なので「復興する」と訳語が合う。

l. 20 …… **Nobusuke Kishi** 岸信介（1896-87）は元総理大臣（任 1957-60）で、安倍晋三総理大臣（任 2006-2007, 2012- ）の祖父。1964 年東京オリンピックを招致した。

l. 21 …… **the event** 2020 年東京オリンピックを指す。

l. 23 …… **deflation** 「デフレ（デフレーション）」。通貨の流通量を縮小してそれに伴って物価が下落すること。経済活動が停滞し、倒産や失業が増大する。

l. 27-28 … **military incursion into China** 「中国への軍事侵略」つまり日中戦争を指している。

l. 30 …… **occupy** （occupied）「占領する」／occupation「（日本の）占領期」。特に 1945 年ポツダム宣言を受け入れてから、1952 年の対日平和条約であるサンフランシスコ講和条約発効までの期間を連合軍（特にアメリカ）による占領期と呼ぶ。

l. 30 …… **the Allied Powers** 第二次世界大戦の連合国。powers には「大国」の意味がある。

l. 35-36 … **Among the many infrastructure projects timed to coincide with the event was the Shinkansen bullet train.** 倒置が起きていて、主語は the Shinkansen bullet train。元々の語順は The Shinkansen bullet train was among the many infrastructure project ... となる。

l. 44 …… **Yoyogi National Gymnasium** 国立代々木競技場。第一体育館や第二体育館などスポーツ施設が複数ある。丹下健三が設計した第一体育館は特徴的な外観で有名。

l. 67 …… **Abebe Bikila** アベベ・ビキラ（1932-73）。エチオピアのマラソン選手で 1960 年ローマオリンピックでも裸足で走って優勝した。

l. 68 …… **Larysa Latynina** ラリサ･ラチニア（1934-）ソ連（現ウクライナ）の体操選手。

Checking Your Understanding: True or False

本文の内容に照らして合っているものにはTを、間違えているものにはFを書きなさい。

1. ___ Tokyo spent the same amount of money as the national budget for the 1964 Olympic Games at that time.

2. ___ The 1940 Tokyo Olympic Games were the first games held in Asia.

3. ___ Haneda Airport was built, timed to coincide with the 1964 Tokyo Olympic Games.

4. ___ We can see many legacies which the 1964 Tokyo Olympic Games brought to the current Tokyo.

How to Read a Paragraph

以下の問いに答えなさい。なお、（ ）内は正解が記述されている段落番号です。

1. なぜ1940年東京オリンピックは中止されたのですか。(Paragraph 5)

____

2. 2020年東京オリンピックにかかる予算が低く抑えられそうなのはどうしてですか。(Paragraph 8)

____

3. 1964年東京オリンピックの時に生まれた「オリンピック景気」という表現を、消費者の目線で具体例を挙げて説明しなさい。(Paragraph 12)

____

Translating into English

Reading Passeges を見ずに、日本語に合うように（　　）内の語句を並び替えて、英文を完成させましょう。冒頭に来る語でも頭文字を小文字にしてあります。

1. 安倍氏はそのイベントがプラスの経済効果を与えることを望んでいる。
   (positive / staging / the / will / Mr. Abe / have / a / hopes / event / economic / impact).

   ____

2. 日本はその戦争に負け、アメリカが主導する連合国によって占領されていた。
   (been / the / by / Allied Powers / had / led / the / war / and / lost / Japan / occupied) the United States.

   ____

3. 増大しつつあった中流階級はオリンピックを見るために TV の受像機を買いに走った。
   (middle / television / growing / rushed / to / sets / Olympics / a / buy / to / watch / class / the).

   ____

Listening Summary

下記の単語から正しいものを選んで空欄を埋めなさい。また、音声を聴いて答えを確認しましょう。なお、冒頭に来る語でも頭文字を小文字にしてあります。

①(　　　　　　　　) the 1964 Tokyo Olympic Games, Japan returned to the ②(　　　　　　　　) stage again. When Tokyo was chosen to host it in 1959, Japan was still ③(　　　　　　　　) from World War II. Mr. Kishi, the Prime Minister at that time believed that it would bring a ④(　　　　　　　　) economic ⑤(　　　　　　　　). In fact, it led to the term "Olympic economy" : we rushed to build many ⑥(　　　　　　　　) and buy household ⑦(　　　　　　　　) such as TV sets.

• appliances • impact • hosting • recovering • global • infrastructures • positive

UNIT

15 New for Valentine's Day in Japan: No Men

バレンタインデーの新潮流

© AFP ＝時事

バレンタインデーは女性（female）から男性（male）へチョコを贈る日だと思っている人は、最近の 2.14 の変化に驚くかもしれない。これまで 2.14 は「本命チョコ」（chocolate for one's significant other）から「義理チョコ」（obligation chocolate）まで夫婦や恋人のみならず、同僚（co-worker）など「男性に感謝を表す日」（a men appreciation day）であった。だが近年、女性が自分へのご褒美（reward for oneself）にチョコを買ったり（自分チョコ）、女友達同士でチョコを贈りあったり（友チョコ）するのが一般的になりつつある。また様々な商業施設では「女子会」の流行にのって女友達同士で楽しむ 2.14 を提案する。

Matching Words & Phrases

次の 1 ～ 10 の語句を、ⓐ ～ⓙの中の最も適切な意味と線で結びましょう。

1. obligation ・　ⓐ 義理
2. survey ・　ⓑ（支持を）表明する
3. favor [動] ・　ⓒ 調査
4. exchange ・　ⓓ …になろうとしている
5. venue ・　ⓔ 代表（者）
6. participant ・　ⓕ …を試みる、企てる
7. attempt ・　ⓖ …を対象とする
8. turn into ... ・　ⓗ …と交換する
9. aim at ・　ⓘ 会場
10. representative ・　ⓙ 参加者、関係者

Reading Passages

1 In Japan, the tradition for Valentine's Day has long been about women giving chocolate to men—the famous "giri choco," or "obligation chocolate." Men are showered with boxes of chocolate from not only their wives and girlfriends, but their female co-workers, friends and daughters, making it more of a "men appreciation day."

2 Now it's turning into a day for women to enjoy themselves, without men.

3 According to a survey by Printemps Ginza, a department store in Tokyo, there has been an increase in women who are enjoying chocolate on Valentine's Day as a reward for themselves. While 61% of women still considered "honmei choco," or chocolate for one's significant other, to be the most important type of chocolate on Valentine's Day, 24% valued chocolate alone, or "jibun choco." (By way of comparison, a year ago, 68% favored homnei, 21% jibun).

4 Women are also enjoying exchanging chocolate among their friends. "Chocolates with cute wrapping and lower prices are very popular this year," Manabu Nudejima, a PR representative at Tokyu Department Store, told JRT. He said that "tomo-choco" (chocolate for friends) is gaining popularity among women.

5 Events and discounts are being designed especially for women on Valentine's Day to enjoy with their friends. L'ala Pado, a women's magazine has planned a "Valentine Day Jyoshi-Kai (Girls' Night)" at the Landmark Square Tokyo in Shinagawa, a venue often used for weddings and banquets. The first half of the event is "a fashion talk about this spring's trends" with a stylist and make-up artists. The second half includes a dinner with beer, wine and cocktails. Participants are told to bring their fashion smart, as the dress code is "your spring fashion."

6 Though the magazine had planned events like this in the past, this is the first time that it has attempted a women-only Valentine's event. "New ways of enjoying chocolate on Valentine's Day, like exchanging with friends, is becoming popular, so we thought we would go along with that concept," Mayuko Kouwaki, an editor at the magazine said. The event

shower［動］:「どっさり与える」
value［動］:「価値のあるものと考える」
by way of comparison:「比較として」
PR:「(public relationsの略)広報活動」
discount:「割引セール」
banquet:「祝宴」
trend:「流行」
bring O ... :「Oを…にする」
go along with ... :「…に賛同する」

has been popular, with more women applying for the event
40 than the 130 spots available.

[7] Hotel Nikko Tokyo, located near the romantic Rainbow Bridge in Odaiba, has created a plan named "Salon du chocolat" just for women to spend an evening together on Valentine's Day. Friends can enjoy a luxurious night in a
45 balcony room complete with chocolate sweets and a bottle of champagne for ¥100,000 and up. However, the plan was not as successful as the hotel had hoped.

[8] In addition, Tokyo Disney Resort has also devoted a page on its "Valentine Nights 2013" event homepage just for
50 women and their friends. This page outlines ways for women to enjoy the Valentine's Day event at Tokyo Disney Sea, originally aimed at couples, as a "limited premium jyoshi-kai." The plan is geared towards women who want to enjoy Valentine's Day at Disney Sea on their way home from work,
55 using the "after-5" passport.

apply for:「…申し込む」
luxurious:「豪華な」
complete with ...:「…が揃った」
and up:「以上」
devote:「(紙面などを)充てる」
outline:「説明する」
originally:「もともとは」
limited:「…限定」
gear:「(計画などに)沿う」

The Keys to Reading Passages

l. 4-5 …… **not only A but (also) B** 「A だけではなく B も」

l. 40 …… **available** 何かが「すぐに使うことが可能、あるいは手に入れることが可能な状態」を指す。the 130 spots available は「(利用可能なのは／用意されているのは) 130 人分の席」という意味になる。Ex. Tickets are available on the day of the game only.「チケットは試合当日のみ発売します。」また、人を修飾する場合は「別の用事が入っておらず、空いている状態」を表す。Ex. Are you available for a meeting now?（今、会議に出てもらえますか？）I'm not available on Monday.「月曜日は［別の用事が入っていて］空いていません。」

l. 54 …… **on one's way home** 「家に帰る途中」on one's way to が基本形。home の前に to が付いていないのは、この場合の home は名詞ではなくて副詞で「家へ」という意味になり、既に方向を示す意味を含んでいるからである。併せて、to（前置詞）のあとに来る目的語は名詞であることを確認しておこう。

Checking Your Understanding: True or False

本文の内容に照らして合っているものには T を、間違えているものには F を書きなさい。

1. ___ "Obligation chocolate" is the tradition for Valentine's Day in Japan.

2. ___ Now Valentine's Day is turning into a day for women to appreciate not only their husbands and boyfriends but also their male co-workers, friends and sons.

3. ___ According to Mayuko Kouwaki, an editor, she planned a women-only Valentine's event, because "Tomo choco" and "Jibun choco" were getting popular.

4. ___ Tokyo Disney Sea has introduced a new way for couples to enjoy Valentine's Day.

How to Read a Paragraph

以下の問いに答えなさい。なお、（　）内は正解が記述されている段落番号です。

1. プランタン銀座の調査によれば、バレンタインデーの楽しみ方として本命チョコより自分チョコを好む割合は、前年度比で何％増えていますか。(Paragraph 3)

____

2. 『ラーラぽど』が企画した「バレンタインデー女子会」の内容を説明しなさい。(Paragraph 5)

____

3. 東京ディズニーリゾートが提案する「バレンタイン・ナイト 2013（限定プレミアム女子会）」が狙いとする対象と、その企画の中身を説明しなさい。(Paragraph 8)

____

Translating into English

Reading Passeges を見ずに、日本語に合うように（　　　）内の語句を並び替えて、英文を完成させましょう。冒頭に来る語でも頭文字を小文字にしてあります。

1. 61% の女性はいまだに本命チョコがバレンタインデーにおいて最も重要なチョコレートの典型だと考えている。
(women / to / type / considered / of / "honmei choco" / most / the / important / of / still / be / chocolate / 61%) on Valentine's Day.

____

2. そのイベントは人気があり、用意された 130 席より多くの女性がそのイベントに申し込んだ。
The event has been popular, (the / more / for / event / women / the / 130 / with / applying / than / spots / available).

____

3. そのプランはそのホテルが期待していたほど成功しなかった。
   (successful / was / as / plan / not / hoped / the / hotel / as / the / had).

   ____

Listening Summary

下記の単語から正しいものを選んで空欄を埋めなさい。また、音声を聴いて答えを確認しましょう。

In Japan, men have long been ①(   ) with chocolate sweets on Valentine's Day such as "giri choco" or "②(   ) chocolate," and "honmei choco" or "chocholate for one's ③(   ) others." However, the number of women who buy chocolate for ④(   ) on Valentine's Day has been increasing recently. Also, ⑤(   ) at women, many companies ⑥(   ) to ⑦(   ) women-only events and discounts now.

• **obligation** • **offer** • **showered** • **significant** • **themselves** • **aiming** • **attempt**

15 Things Happening in Japan:
From <A Hit Drama "Hanzawa Naoki"> to <Yoshitomo Nara's New Life>
日本で起きている15のあらゆること
――〈ドラマ『半沢直樹』ヒットの要因〉から〈奈良美智の再生と「成長」〉まで

2015年4月10日　初版第1刷発行
2016年4月20日　第2版第1刷発行

編著者　宮本　文

発行者　森　信久
発行所　**株式会社　松 柏 社**
〒102-0072　東京都千代田区飯田橋1-6-1
TEL 03 (3230) 4813（代表）
FAX 03 (3230) 4857
http://www.shohakusha.com
e-mail: info@shohakusha.com

装　丁　小島トシノブ（NONdesign）
本文レイアウト　株式会社クリエーターズ・ユニオン（一柳　茂）
印　刷　シナノ書籍印刷株式会社
ISBN978-4-88198-707-0
略号＝707